I0149185

UNDERSTANDING DESTINY

The Story of Ruth and God's Blueprint for Fulfilling Destiny

STEWART MBA

Published by KHARIS PUBLISHING, an imprint of
KHARIS MEDIA LLC

Copyright © 2016 Stewart Mba

ISBN: 10: 1-946277-00-2
ISBN-13: 978-1-946277-00-8

All rights reserved. This book or parts thereof may not be
reproduced in any form, stored in a retrieval system, or
transmitted in any form by any means - electronic, mechanical,
photocopy, recording, or otherwise - without prior written
permission of the publisher, except as provided by United States
of America copyright law.

Unless otherwise stated, all scriptural quotations are from the
King James Version (KJV)

All KHARIS PUBLISHING products are available at special
quantity discounts for bulk purchase for sales promotions,
premiums, fund-raising, and educational needs. For details, write:

Kharis Media LLC
709 SW Elmside Drive
Bentonville,
AR 72712
Tel: 479-599-8657
info@kharispublishing.com
www.kharispublishing.com

DEDICATION

To the Holy Spirit

CONTENTS

ACKNOWLEDGMENTS

My sincere appreciation goes to the following: my precious wife and co-laborer in the vineyard; Aderomola, and the entire members of the Priesthood Assembly who had the courage to participate in this publication after hearing the message of destiny exposed at church.

I want to also mention baby Destiny Bombata whose mother, in her pregnancy, was inspired by the message of destiny and, therefore, named her after this subject: Destiny, indeed. She is already one of the gracious products of this work on the account of her miraculous birth experience. Praise God.

And, of course, all those who indirectly were also part of it. Truly, vision is given to a man, but it takes many to execute. Glory to God. Amen.

INTRODUCTION

Destiny is one concept in life that is either misunderstood or barely understood by many people. Consequently, the effort by many well-meaning individuals has either been deflected, frustrated, or even destroyed. The scripture declares vividly in Hosea 4:6, "my people are destroyed for lack of knowledge…"

The sad reality is that hopes and lives have been wasted, and many are facing impending despair resulting from the lack of understanding of destiny.

Although the concept of destiny is in popular use, it has not been fundamentally explored. There are many messages on fulfilling destiny or discovering destiny, and yet there is little or no clear understanding of its profound meaning and basis. Unfortunately, it is practically impossible to fulfill, achieve, or satisfy an expectation that is not known.

The earth is disproportionately full of striving or struggling men and women who, unfortunately, are ignorant of the harmonious ingredients that destiny brings to make life meaningful. Without the understanding of destiny, life's endeavors ultimately have no meaning.

It is my strong belief that this short work will provide clear and significant insight into your destiny.

I have no doubt whatsoever that this simple scripture-based exposition on destiny will release and liberate many from unnecessary struggles and aimless lives.

The whole concept of destiny is implicitly embedded in the Bible, although it is not directly expressed or mentioned in the bible – especially if you are one of those fine folks who are used to the King James Version.

Prompted by an enduring revelation and burdened by the conflict and confusion apparent in an unfulfilled and powerless life, evident in much suffering and anxiety faced by many people, I yield myself to be used by God for this task. However, to achieve God's desired mind in this work, one must read and absorb this book with an open, humble, and sincere heart that is receptive and adaptive to God. This is indeed my honest submission. Thus, this work is broken into two main sections: the first section deals with understanding destiny, while the second section deals with practical suggestions from the bible on how to fulfill destiny.

My sincere prayer is that you will find this piece of work an enablement and a source of peace and joy in fulfilling your destiny. You are encouraged to study all the bible passages that are referenced in this book. And, of course, faithfully proclaim over your life the prayerful declarations that conclude some of these chapters.

To God be all the glory. Amen.

PART ONE
INTRODUCTION

It's possible to work hard and be full of vision but without understanding of destiny, there may never be fulfillment and power. Hence, it is not just enough to have a vision, destiny must first be understood.

The concept of "understanding" here implies the power of clear thought or intelligence (this is not just having knowledge of a vision but embracing the vision in line with God's will). Having a clear thought further involves a mind that is devoid of negative or strange influences toward life and set goals. Destiny must be understood to give life divine meaning. Proverbs 16:22 says, "Understanding is a wellspring of life to him who has it." Further, Proverbs 2:11 says, "discretion will preserve you; understanding will keep you." Understanding goes beyond knowledge and wisdom. Proverbs 3:19 says: "The Lord by wisdom has founded the earth; by understanding He has established the heavens."

Beyond knowledge and wisdom, we need understanding. Solomon asked God for understanding, and God was pleased with him in regards to his request and, in addition, gave him wisdom and riches (1 Kings 3: 9-13, 4:29) because wisdom is the key to understanding (Proverbs 4:5). While wisdom is the application of knowledge, understanding is the power of clear thought for an efficient and skillful result and judgement.

The Spirit of God is an embodiment of knowledge, wisdom, and understanding (Ex. 31:3). Generally, they go in this graduating order: data to information, information to knowledge, knowledge to understanding, and, finally, understanding to wisdom. We know this from Proverbs 4:7, which reads, "Wisdom is the principal thing; therefore get wisdom; and with all thy getting get understanding."

Understanding is of utmost importance to destiny. God desires and makes every provision for us to have understanding of our destinies (Jer. 3:15). And, like the Psalmist who said, "Give me understanding and I shall keep thy law," we must seek and crave for understanding (Ps. 119:34).

No wonder in Matthew 15:16, Jesus enquired: "Are you also yet without understanding?" May God open our eyes to understand this embedded and implied relational message of destiny (Luke 24:45). Amen.

~~~

We must have advanced understanding of destiny indeed. 1 Corinthians 14: 2 says "Brethren, be not be children in understanding…" Apostle Paul toiled and struggled in the religion of his fathers (Acts 22, Gal. 1:13-14). Saul struggled without fulfillment until he received the understanding of his destiny. We read in Acts of this fulfillment: "suddenly there shined round about him a light from heaven and on laying on of his hands of Ananias…immediately there fell down his eyes as it had been scales, and he received sight (*understanding*) forthwith and arose…" (Acts 9: 1-3, 17-18 [emphasis added]).

In that moment, destiny was aligned, and Saul, now Paul, never again conferred with flesh and blood but began genuine exploits according to God's plan for his life . He writes, "when it pleased God…to reveal his son in me, that I might preach him among the hearten: immediately I conferred not with flesh and blood…" (Gal 1: 15-17). When destiny is not understood, there is always the tendency of relying on men or earthly power for direction.

Truly, without understanding destiny, there can never be fulfillment and power, irrespective of human exertion, determination, acquisitions, or possessions. Jesus Christ understood His destiny – His life on earth was purely driven by the consciousness of this understanding. Matthew 1:21, speaking of Christ's destiny, says: "For he shall save His people from their sin", and Luke 2:34 declares that Jesus "is set (destined) for the fall and rising again of many in Israel…" (emphasis added).

Because He knew his destiny, He submitted Himself to baptism, resisted temptations, and gave Himself to service as we see in Matthew 3:13 -17, 4:1, 4:12 and John 4: 31 – 34, 9:4.

On these accounts, He was able to foretell His betrayer (Jn. 13: 21 – 27), spoke of His leaving and the coming comforter (Jn. 16: 4-7), and protected His disciples (Jn. 18: 1-9) by not transferring or imposing His affliction, burden, or personal responsibility on them, "For every man shall bear his own burden" (Gal. 6:5).

Note that "burden", as in Gal. 6:2, "Bear ye one another's burdens…" means "baros" in Greek, which translates to moral weakness. At the same time, "burden" has a different meaning in Galatians 6:5, as it means here in Greek, "phortion" – personal responsibility. While we are encouraged to bear one another's moral weakness, every man is to bear his own personal responsibility, as it is often tantamount to fulfilling destiny. For instance, while we might help others to overcome poverty, we are not expected to carry the responsibility of such poverty. I can help someone in their training but the responsibility for his failure or success is his alone.

When they came to arrest and, consequently, kill Him, Jesus could have taken the advantage of the fact that the Jews that came to arrest him had difficulty identifying and distinguishing him from the rest of His disciples. He could have used that occasion to transfer the havoc to His disciples. This would have impeded God's plan for Him. Instead, He emphatically protected them and, therefore, exempted them from the share of His personal responsibility or affliction. Jesus also was not deterred by threats, saying: "destroy this temple (His body), and in three days I will raise it up" and, of course, He worked and accomplished His father's work on earth (Jn. 4:35, 9:4).

In like manner, only those who understand destiny can submit themselves to divine will, resist temptations, and give themselves to service. Those who understand destiny will always have an apparent ability to predict enemies, are conscious of divine exit, and will never transfer personal responsibilities to others. They carry their own crosses (Matt. 10:38).

Oftentimes, people frustrate their own destinies by merely running away from certain responsibilities or challenges. And, by putting it on others, they are never tested and promoted in life.

Similarly, men and women of destiny are not deterred by threat and are ready to accomplish a given task to its logical conclusion.

Now, in case you're reading this book and you're not yet born again or have not yet surrendered your life to Jesus Christ, accept that destiny is of God our creator. If you are in disobedience or disagreement to His will, you can never understand and fulfill destiny. Amos 3:3 says, "…two cannot work together except they be agreed." Sin is a form of disobedience and disagreement against God. Be ready to confess and repent of your sins today. That way, you are graciously bound to understand and fulfill your destiny.

Would you pray the following prayer of repentance with me today?

Father, I come to you now as a sinner and ask for your forgiveness and mercy; cleanse me with the blood of your son, Jesus Christ, whom I confess today as your only begotten son. Thank you for saving me.

Congratulations, and may you never lack understanding of your destiny. Amen.

In conclusion, please join me in the following prayer of declaration:

Father, I proclaim light from heaven against every

strange thing that has blinded me against my destiny. I hereby receive a clear understanding of my destiny today. In Jesus name. Amen.

DEFINITION AND BACKGROUND ANALYSIS

Destiny, in its simple definition, means a future which has been decided or planned at an earlier time.

It's indeed functionally the power (authority, influence, or force) believed to control events of life. Thus, to be destined implies having a future which has been decided in advance. Now, there are General and Specific destinies. The General involves our common likeness and image of God, which applies to all. It is in the Specific that we differ. This is an important clarification about destiny. The latter is a part and derivative of the former. Without the former, the latter is impossible; they are integral to one another. Our study is, however, centered on the Specific destiny.

First, a brief review of General Destiny, which is common to all believers.

An outright play of our General destiny is revealed and buttressed in God's creation statement in the book of Genesis. This, we can fundamentally use to first elaborate our definition.

"And God said, let us make man in our image, after our likeness: and let them have dominion over the fish of the sea, and over the fowl of the air, and over the cattle, and over all the earth.... So God created man in his own image, in the image of God created he him ... And God blessed them, and God said unto them, be fruitful and multiply replenish the earth, and subdue it: and have dominion over the fish of the sea, and over living things that move upon the earth" (Gen. 1: 26-28).

From the assertion of this passage, there was a future which was decided upon prior to the creation of human beings. In verse 26, there was a decision to make human beings, in association with other elemental factors. Consequently, in verse 27, the creation took place directly on the basis of the specification of that which was decided upon, implying that the latter was controlled by the former.

Thus, the power that controlled the creation of man in verse 27 was God's word (plan/power) in verse 26. Indeed His word is powerful (Heb. 4:12).

God had a plan on which the basis of creation took place. This is exactly what Paul, by the Holy Spirit, buttressed in the recreation experience in Ephesians 2:10. Reading from the Amplified version of the Bible:

"For we are God's [own] handiwork [His workmanship], recreated in Christ Jesus, [born anew] that we may do those good works which God predestined [planned beforehand] for us [taking paths] which He prepared ahead of time, that we should walk in them [living the good life which He pre-arranged and made ready for us to live]."

The study of Roman 8:29 reveals that the concepts of predestination or destiny of humans is the belief that certain things that happen now, like the death and resurrection of Christ, and redemption opportunity for humanity, have really been decided in advance by God. Truly, the work of God today is the direct product of His thought or plan yesterday or prior to the event or performance (details of this are provided in the subsequent part).

We must, at this point, realize that the goal of predestination is not a divine predetermined plan to send some to hell and others to heaven as some erroneously believe and, therefore, have consciously or unconsciously given up on the good side of life. This has no biblical backing at all. God's plan or desire is not for any person to fall or go to hell except if the person so chooses (1 Tim 2:34; 2 Pet 3:9).

God's plan, as fundamentally seen in Genesis 1:26, was to make human beings in His image and for them to subdue and have dominion over every other creature as well as to become worshippers of God. This, accordingly, becomes God's plan and mandate for humans without exception. Thus, God does not destine any to fail or end up in hell; it's a matter of choice. Every individual has the ability and responsibility to repent and be conformed to his original plan (destiny).

Scripture declares that every good thing comes from God. He has for everyone, including Judas Iscariot, a thought of good and to bring us to an expected end; otherwise, grace is of no effect. Grace is God's unmerited goodness toward individuals, without exception. It is truly unmerited favor to be counted worthy of heaven through repentance and righteousness, instead deserved hell.

Foreknowledge vs. Destiny

Further, in Romans 8:28-30 and Ephesians 1:5, the term "foreknowledge" speaks of God's awareness of the potential future. Study Acts 2:23. This must not be confused with destiny. Understand that God's foreknowledge of an event or an occurrence in life does not imply He planned or decided it. Therefore, this must not be confused with destiny. As a result, it is wrong to believe and accept, like the Muslim religion for instance, that whatever happens to a man—be it positive or negative—has been destined by God. That God foreknows does not mean He planned it. This is the same as when we falsely think that since God foreknows the result of certain wrong decisions we make, He could stop those decisions. That's quite erroneous as that would, of course, negate the human power of choice.

In a nutshell, destiny is the plan of a person's life, a blueprint which has been thought about in detail in advance, - to be executed based on a prototype or specification (a reference working file). What life becomes depends on the execution of divine plan (destiny). This definition will serve as our working definition and overall platform for the rest of our studies on destiny in this book.

Suffice it to say that we live in the days where men and women have misconstrued money or riches as the goal of destiny, that fulfilling destiny entails the amount of money one has acquired. Far from it. A fulfilled destiny does not consist of the abundance of a person's possessions but the fulfillment in life on earth according to God's prior plan for you. It is sad, but true, that some have fallaciously striven after money, without really fulfilling God's real plan for their lives.

~~~~

The path of destiny is peace and joy, and these are indicators of a fulfilling or fulfilled destiny and not merely material possessions, which tend to be accompanied by sorrow, fear, and uneasy living. The crave for riches has, at the expense of destiny, driven people to high desire of materialism and fame at all costs and by all means. This sad state can only be defused by understanding the true meaning of destiny. A person's ultimate and real achievement in life directly lies in fulfilling destiny and never just on the magnitude of temporal possessions. Obviously, there are many Christians who are destined as leaders but may not necessarily be wealthy. And, of course, to be a leader often involves a measure of contented material life.

The greatest tragedy in life, I think, is operating outside one's own destiny, of individuals belonging to or pursuing "un-destined" careers, missions, or professions. For example, I once asked a lady why she was studying banking and finance at her university. Her answer indicated that there was no relationship between her destiny and her choice of course of study. She just wanted to study such a course to make money in life. Just like many others, she probably will never experience fulfillment and inner empowerment no matter what, no matter how far she climbs the proverbial career ladder. Some years ago, I encountered a young Christian brother who came to tell me how he had failed a national/regional university entrance examination, brilliant as he was. As a pastor by the grace of God, and having known him closely for a while, I realized he failed because his choice of subjects were not in agreement with his perceived destiny. Consequently, I advised him on a new line of subjects, which he eventually accepted. He sat for the examination, passed the papers, was admitted, and has now graduated. Praise God.

May I conclude here by stressing that "purpose" is not "destiny", per se. Purpose is mainly an essential part of destiny or one of the many parts of destiny. Destiny is more than purpose. The concept of destiny cannot, therefore, be reduced to a mere ideology of purpose. Purpose is basically "an aim" or "reason for doing." I would argue that destiny goes beyond reason, it encompasses the reason, make-up, content, and extent of a person's life (the entire blueprint) – for both individuals or a group. To define or use purpose as destiny, in my mind, is to narrow down drastically the entire concept of destiny and limit a profound revelation that could change our lives. So, may I suggest that your read the rest of this book with an open mind.

Prayerful Declaration:

Father, I declare that my future has been determined by you, and, therefore, cannot be controlled by mere circumstances and situations. In Jesus' name.

DESTINY AND THE POWER OF CHOICE

God's initiative and work in humans was directly aimed at fulfilling destiny. Hence, humans are a product of destiny. The Bible says we are called according to His purpose (destiny) (Rom. 8:28b). He puts everything in the perfect order of destiny. We are fearfully and beautifully made and He makes everything beautiful in its time (Ecc. 3:11). He made us, and He called us good (Gen 1:31).

We are God's handwork or workmanship. In other words, we are systematically formed in a specified way (Gen 2:7).

The word "make" is a verb used to reflect workmanship; in the same way the word "formed" in Genesis 2:7 is expressive of craftsmanship. To "make" denotes construction; to construct, therefore, is to combine materials or parts together. This evokes a similar imagery as in the building of the tabernacle or the Ark of Noah (Gen. 1:26-28, 6:14-22; Ex. 25:8, 10, 26:1).

Every individual is made or created with the ability to fulfill destiny. Besides our common destiny, everyone is designed for a specific and uncommon destiny. God knows what every person should become in life. He destined every man for a specific accomplishment. Therefore, He has made (and still makes) available to us all that is required to become who He has destined us to be. Is there a reason God chose to make every other creation before creating a human being? Could it be because He wants to evaluate what is available, and then determine what else needs to be fitted into a human being in order to fulfill destiny? A useful product is one that is produced only after a need is identified. It is afterward produced with the ability to satisfy the identified need.

God could not have desired Isaac through the womb of Sarah if He hadn't put in her the ability to conceive. In her was every resource needed to bring forth Isaac. It was just a matter of faith. Of course, things may be marred by other forces, but God will yet amend them so that destiny can be accomplished. We can be remolded by Him to fit into our destinies. A critical study of a symbolic bible lesson from the potter's house reveals this:

> *"The word which Came to Jeremiah from the Lord saying, Arise, and go down to the potter's house, and there I will cause thee to hear my words. Then I went down to the potter's house, and, behold, he wrought a work on the wheels. And the vessel that he made of clay was marred in the hand of the potter: so he made it again another. Then the word of the Lord came to me, saying, O house of Israel, cannot I do with you as this potter? Saith the Lord. Behold, as the clay is in the potter's hand so are ye in mine hand, O house of Israel"* *(Jer 18: 1-6).*

You may not have presently accomplished

everything you desire, because God is yet amending a certain marred ability in your life, you may yet be enabled to fulfill your destiny. He can, and He is perfecting it, as seems good to Him and your destiny. Don't give up; yield yourself to Him.

You're designed to be a "round peg in a round hole." As long as you are tied to your destiny, you must never struggle to be what you are not; no matter the era of life – marriage, career etc. You must always experience a steady advancement in life. Refuse to be humanly re-shaped. He made you a good fit for your destiny.

Noah's Ark was made to accomplish its predetermined purpose and expectations. Its capacity and durability were carefully preplanned. The windows were for light and ventilation. The three stories were to separate the animals for safety and cooperation during the voyage. All these were made available on the basis of its expected use. The size of 95,700 square feet deck space was for it to be able to convey the big carriage. God has, in like manner, made in us the capacity to withstand every challenge in life. As God was mindful of the strength and height needed for the ark to stay above water for 371 days, so also, He has made in us every suitable and lasting strength we need to live and fulfill destiny. It took quite a lot of resources and time to build the ark in order to stand the test of time. It took a stretch of 170 years to build the ark, so also you are not a product of haste.

Man is systematically and tactically made and assigned to an uncommon destiny. You are not made to expire until you fulfill your destiny. Sarah's womb may have gone dead by human evaluation and yet that never incapacitated the bringing forth of Isaac. You will surely finish the race in honor and glory.

The truth remains that whatever becomes of our human induced inability cannot be capable of overriding the fulfillment of our destiny. We are created and born with every potential ability to fulfill destiny. And, if in the process of life on earth, certain human inabilities emerge through socialization, inheritance, or strange forces of the enemy, we can as well have them changed or amended by God to conform to His original designs for us. If the automobile builder can humanly replace any defected part of its product for efficient operational fulfillment, then God is more than able and willing to replace any part in us to help us fulfill our destinies. Destiny is fundamental to existence and calling. This is, once again, God's revelation to Jeremiah. Our sincere consciousness of this foundational revelation will strengthen us and completely disarm the devil against our destinies. Halleluiah!!

The word of the Lord came to Jeremiah and said that before He *"formed thee in the belly I knew thee; and before thou camest forth out of the womb I sanctified thee, and I ordained thee a prophet unto the nations. Then said I ah, Lord God! Behold I cannot speak: for I am a child"* (Jer. 1 : 4-6).

Paul, after conversion, came to terms personally with this *revelational* reality, saying, "But when it pleased God, who separated me from my mother's womb, and called me by his grace" (Gal 1:15).

This truly does not only apply to Jeremiah and Paul alone – it is the whole issue of destiny. Since our destinies are of God, and not man, then nothing is capable of aborting them. Every other factor that arises afterward cannot be capable of changing that which was first put in place: destiny. Destiny supersedes Jeremiah's humanly perceived speech and childhood challenges. As terrible as the sin of Adam and Eve was, it could only distort, but not completely destroy, the fulfillment of the destiny of humankind until the restoration of all things by Christ. This suggests, then, that there is no being or force capable of destroying our God-given destiny if we cooperate with God. If man repents, then fulfillment of his destiny still awaits him.

If God commanded Noah and Moses, in regards to the ark and tabernacle respectively, to build according to His plan or specification, then He can also never drift from His original plan or destiny for human creation. He will always perform whatever He resolves. Our destinies are no exception. After the fall of man in Adam, God again restored man to His original plan through His Son, Jesus Christ (Rom 5:12-21; 1 Cor 15:21-23).

God also created a unique destiny for each person. For "whom He did foreknow, he also did predestine" (Rom 8:29). Every destiny is unique, uncommon, and unprecedented. Therefore, we must not envy or be intimidated but someone else's social status or progress, just as we must not despise any other person's weakness, reproach, or state of challenges at any given time, for we are, in life, blessed or affected at different times, ways, and places by God in line with our destinies as they unfold. No one should be judged or discarded until he or she dies or Christ comes. An amazing thing with destiny is that it's not over until it's over. And, of course, we have no need as humans to unduly compete or compare ourselves one to another. Destinies never compete nor are they comparable (2 Cor 10:12, Gal 6:4).

Christians who directly or indirectly intimidate others with their material testimonies at a given time really don't understand destiny. There are times when it can be silent or invisible, and there are times when it can be loud or visible by way of material perspectives. There is always a stage of testimony or progress per time in every man that operates in God's will – it may be a building or planting time for one, and for another, a reaping or harvesting time, and vice versa. What we are today is not an entire value of our lives. I believe that one of the mistakes of Paul in ministry was the way he judged the young John Mark rather harshly (Acts 15: 37-39). The fact that Mark was at a particular phase in his journey in life and ministry that made him temporarily abandon Paul and Silas did not mean that he could never be useful ministry material. Thank God that Silas looked beyond Mark's immediate mistakes and saw a larger destiny looming ahead of the young man. Years later, even Paul himself had to acknowledge that John Mark had been "useful to me in ministry" (Tim 4:11).

We must not only learn from the successes of the Apostles; we can also learn from their mistakes. While Mark was rejected by Paul, Barnabas held on to him. Eventually, the same John Mark became essential to Paul in the work of the ministry while Paul was in prison. And, of course, John Mark became the writer of the second gospel in the New Testament.

DESTINY AND CHOICE

I do not believe that the destiny of any individual continually changes. The problem has always been human choice in life, as it affects its fulfillment. Destiny and God's ability to fulfill in an individual is never in doubt – this must be taken much more seriously than ever. Destiny is of God, but choice is of man. While destiny is the power believed to control events of life, choice remains an essential factor on the part of man in the fulfillment of his destiny. Choice, by a simple definition, is an act of choosing between two or more options or possibilities. It is paramount. Man must not stay in-between opinions as far as destiny is concerned. In this instance, the prophet Elijah was quite uncomfortable with Ahab's indecisive attitude.

Thus, he enquired of him; "…how long halt ye between opinions" (1 Kings 18:21). King Ahab was faltering or hovering between two opinions. There is never neutrality in opinion – it's either positive or negative. God created us in His image and likeness and gave us qualities that He possessed. One of which is that He created humans with a will and power of choice. God did not give His power to any other of His creatures except some angelic beings. The angel

Lucifer had this ability, which he consequently misused. He abused and dishonored this power of choice God has granted man. A critical study of the following verses of the scripture reveals great things in this regard.

> "And the Lord God commanded the man, saying of every tree of the garden thou mayest freely eat. But of the tree of the knowledge of good and evil, thou shalt not eat for in the da that thou eatest thereof thou shalt surely die" (Gen. 2: 16-17)

From this passage it is understandable that God accorded to Adam and Eve the privilege of choice. He presented them with all the options and gave them permission to make their choice. However, in His love, He pointed out to them the consequences of certain choices and urged them to choose well.

God advises individuals to choose life instead of death. Everyone can and must make the right choice in order to fulfill destiny. God does not force His will on humanity. This truth is reinforced in Deuteronomy, in which God's people are called to choose life against all other choices (Deut. 30:15, 19).

Without exception, every person is free to choose between life and death, blessing or curse. Hence, from this Deuteronomy scripture we can assert that God presented to man in the garden both good and evil, death and life, while also admonishing man to reject the latter. And, of course, man was fully conscious of his God-given power of choice. The devil himself knows about this. No wonder in Genesis chapter three, Satan in his deception emphasized the lie that God had restricted humanity's freedom of choice in the garden, a clever ploy to appeal to their ego and, therefore, incite them against God.

He centered on this so called restriction, therefore, casting doubt on God's word intentionally, while refusing to declare the fact that God had first said they might freely eat of all the trees. Often times, the devil will want to use our God-given privileges to deceive and destroy us, especially when one is duly overwhelmed by it or allows pride to set in. Lucifer himself is a good example. Sometimes our greatest enemy may just, unfortunately, be the good things we possess. In providing man a "help meet," we can see God's outright demonstration of man's God-given freedom of choice at work (Gen. 2:18-20). The choice of a wife was man's exclusive privilege. A right choice can grant us God's provision and release. This also was what exactly took place in Genesis 2:21-25 when Adam ultimately got the bone of his bone and the flesh of his flesh. This is the power of choice in the face of destiny. Choice is principally a reflection of liberty. God does not compel us to serve Him. Instead, we are called to freedom (Gal. 5:13). To worship and serve Him is a matter of choice (Josh 24:15b).

Covenant servants of God are those who are in service of the Lord because they chose to be when He called. God does not force anyone to serve Him, but rather He compels one who has chosen to serve (Ex. 21:5-6). He gave His son freely, and the son gave Himself by choice. Jonah's encounter with God must not be regarded as an attempt by God to compel Jonah to serve. It was rather a matter of God enforcing the choice Jonah had already made to accept the office, responsibilities, and privileges of a Prophet of God. We have the choice to answer God's call.

Now, the Bible declares that where the spirit of the Lord is, there is liberty (2 Cor 3:17). Liberty is expressed in the power of choice. Hence, while God's presence was in the garden, liberty existed and, consequently, the exercise of the power of choice by Adam and Eve in the garden. Liberty brings about freedom of choice and, subsequently, joy; since where the presence of the Lord is, there is fullness of joy.

God was indeed in the garden with Adam and Eve, desiring to be truly worshipped (Gen. 3:8-9). For true worship to exist, there must be options for and against worship. That is why the Lord possibly placed the tree of life along with the tree of the knowledge of good and evil in the garden, as true obedience can be determined only if an option to disobey is available. Have you ever wondered or pondered on this? There might not have been a true test of obedience without the option to disobey. It's a test of faithfulness. Freedom is essential to true worship and obedience. Without freedom of choice on the side of man, he becomes an object of slavery or bondage. When obedience or worship is under compulsion, it becomes mechanical and devoid of the work or leading of the Holy Spirit.

Does God, who created humanity, not have the power to compel people to do His will, especially to be born again? Of course yes, but that would negate our God-given power or freedom of choice. There is this natural satisfaction in man when permitted to exercise the liberty to choose. The conscience of humans tends to be more responsive when it's free to choose. The preference of democracy to dictatorship is a matter of the freedom of choice. Democracy is preferred basically because of sheer freedom of choice. Churches that force members directly or indirectly to religiously remain in confinement to their denominations or activities will never get the best form of their genuine and sincere worship and service. When they are well-fed and cared for without manipulating them to stay, the genuine ones will certainly stay. Even if any of them leave, there is always the likelihood of them coming back sooner or later.

The emergence of Lucifer on earth as a competing kingdom to the glorious kingdom of God brought another option of choice to man, as there will always be a counter offer by the devil or its human agents. However, the choice is ours. Obviously, in fulfilling destiny, life will always present us with options. What matters is our ability to choose wisely.

In addition, the material and immaterial (physical and spiritual) dual nature of human beings poses yet another challenge of choice to destiny. The problem, therefore, lies in the trials and temptations we face in the midst of our dual nature, as we seek to exercise the power of choice. Further, man is, in life, confronted with two options or alternative "wills": the will of the flesh (physical) and, of course, the "will" of God (spiritual) (Jn. 1:13; Acts 21:14).

Scripture explains Paul's experience in the struggles of these dual natures, which may ultimately lead to evil choices (Rom 7:13 – 25; Gal 5:17).

Jesus Christ was Himself confronted by these,

and if He had opted for the wrong choice of "will," then the eternal salvation and hope of humanity would have been halted abruptly (Lk. 22:42).

While destiny may not compel choice, as it were, the choice made may make or mar its fulfillment (Gen. 13:11). Understand that man was meant to live forever; however, the mere choice of Adam and Eve momentarily frustrated it (Gen. 2:17; 3:22). God is not unaware of this strong and decisive challenge to choose. Hence, He gave human beings a "will" (the mental power by which one can direct his/her thoughts, actions, and influence). Our willpower implies that we possess mental control that can be used over our own impulses as it affects one's choices. Being created in God's likeness includes His kind of mind. Philippians 2:5 declares, "Let this mind be in you which was also in Christ." Furthermore, 1 Corinthians 2:16 explains that "we have the mind of Christ." This simply means that, as Christians, we can reflect God's thoughts, opinions or judgements. Note that after conversion, the mind is subjected to a process of renewal to conform to its original state (Rom. 12:2).

We must all know that whatever God offers has a likelihood of being opposed by Satan through human error. Often times, satanic or human oppositional offers will seem to be better outwardly. This was part of the antics of the devil in the fall of man (Gen. 3). We must be extremely careful in settling for any option or choice. Our choices can make or mar our destiny's fulfillment. Wrong choices regarding a life partner, for example, can frustrate the fulfillment of one's destiny. We must not, at any time, be misled by a variety of options before us. It should not call for pride or confusion but rather carefulness. It may just be a satanic plot. For instance, a lady became so full of herself because of many men who were approaching her for marriage. Rather than being a reason for vain glory, the seriousness of having several options at the same time should call for sober, thoughtful, and prayerful deliberation. It is time to take seriously the privilege of choice that we have been given. Sadly, this particular lady ended up making a wrong choice and, consequently, became a divorcee in no time.

The impact of wrong choices may not be felt immediately. Sometimes, it may even seem like the right decision, but sooner or later, it will backfire (Prov. 14:12).

As Christians, we must understand that certain choices may have permanent consequences for life. This calls for handling our power of choice carefully and prayerfully on a day by day basis.

FACTORS THAT MAY LEAD TO NEGATIVE CHOICES

Let us now consider certain factors that can lead to negative choices that may counter our destiny fulfillment. Some of these factors include notable satanic plots and strategies used in his temptation against Jesus Christ Himself (Luke 4).

1. Deception:

This is one of the greatest tools of the devil especially in this present time.

"For such are false apostles, deceitful workers, transforming themselves into the Apostles of Christ. And no marvel. For Satan himself is transformed into an angel of light. Therefore it is no great thing if his ministers also be transformed as the ministers of righteousness, whose end shall be according to their works" (1 Cor. 11: 13-15).

"For there shall arise false Christ, and false prophets, and shall show great signs and wonders, in so much that, if it were possible they shall deceive the very elect" (Matt. 24:24).

"Now the serpent was more subtle (deceptive) than any beast of the field which the Lord God had made, and he said unto the woman…" (Gen. 3:1 with emphasis).

Satanic power of deception was fundamentally behind the fall of man (Gen. 3). Eve was deceived into making a wrong choice. Before her in the garden were the options "to eat" or "not to eat" the forbidden fruit. She opted for the former based on the force of deception of the agent of devil–the serpent. The Bible says that the serpent was greatly subtle. Its plot was organized in a most clever and complex way, leading to deceit and, consequently, a wrong choice and aborted destiny fulfillment. This strange machinery is still being used by the devil. 2 Corinthians 11:3 tells us that just as Eve was tempted, "so your minds should be corrupted" in the same way.

Refuse to be deceived. Be sensitive in the spirit.

They come in mere cosmetic looks; wolves in sheep clothing. Be warned.

2. Helpless and Sorrowful Situations:

Helpless times are as real as their temporary nature. We all are bound to face negative situations in life. But for believers, it is never meant or permitted by God to destroy us. The devil may take advantage of it to present a conflicting option that, if carelessly considered, is capable of aborting destiny fulfillment.

Orpah and Ruth were together faced by these helpless situational options: to stay with Naomi or depart from her. While Orpah left, Ruth chose to stay. Consequently, Ruth's choice to remain with Naomi, despite all odds, led to her becoming an ancestress of David and Jesus Christ (Matt. 1:15). Through this, she kept the path of destiny. Only men who set their hands on the plow and look not for the things that are behind can fulfill destiny (Lk. 9:62).

No doubt Orpah chose to leave because of the apparent helpless and sorrowful situation. We must not allow helpless situations to negatively influence our choices. We can still make the right choice in helpless situations. Moses, the Bible says, chose to suffer affliction with the people of God, rather than to enjoy the pleasures of sin for a season (Heb. 11:24-26). Orpah chose to go back home to free herself from the affliction she was experiencing with Naomi, her mother-in-law. Ruth, on the other hand, just like Moses did, chose to remain in the affliction with Naomi, whose pain was so much that she had changed her name to 'Mara' (bitterness), instead of 'Naomi' (pleasant). Pain can do that to us – lead us to the place where we tend to allow trails, difficulties, and pain to define us. But, in the midst of it all, Ruth realized that helpless circumstances are temporary.

The ultimate result of a positive choice in a helpless situation is enormous. By faith, we must, like Ruth and Moses, esteem the reproach of Christ more greatly than the treasures in our Moab and Egypt, respectively. Helpless and sorrowful situations at any point in time must not influence us to wrong choices. You may have stressfully awaited for the right life partner. Wait for the right choice. Jesus Christ opted for the choice of the will of His father even when His soul was overwhelmed with sorrow, and destiny was fulfilled (Matt. 26:38-39).

3. Lust of the Flesh:

While in wilderness, the devil desired to take advantage of Christ's severe human hunger for food after a stretch of 40 days of fasting (Matt 4:1-2). In the same way, the enemy also tempts us in times of hunger into making wrong choices. He always seeks to get the advantage over us when we are under pressure and puts us on the spot to gratify or satisfy the flesh.

Due to hunger, Esau opted to sell his birthright to his brother. His choice of food instead of his birthright was induced by hunger – desiring to satisfy the flesh. Eve's lust of the eyes led to the wrong choice. In the face of hunger, we must not make a choice that would deviate us from fulfilling our destinies.

4. Stinginess:

Stinginess is the unwillingness to give or unsacrificial giving, resulting in careless and thoughtless offerings, like that of Cain. The contrast between Cain and Abel was not between an offering of plant life and an offering of animal life, but between a choice of a careless offering by Cain and a choice of a generous offering by Abel. Stinginess can abort destiny fulfillment. Cain derailed his destiny because of his unsacrificial offering. A man that is destined to be rich can have his destiny fulfillment frustrated by his own sheer will of stinginess or miserly habits. Cain's offering of plants was not the real case against him. It was a matter of quality giving. This revelation is made relevant on the account that Abel's offering was "more excellent" (Heb. 11:4), possibly because it was the right kind of offering, as it was made with a generous and sacrificial intention of his heart.

5. Greed:

Greed somehow differs from stinginess. It has to do with an excessive desire for wealth, power etc., for one's self – without consideration for the needs of other people or at the expenses of others. As far as Abraham's conflict with Lot was concerned, Abraham never gave in to greed, as would have been naturally expected, since he made Lot rich. His self-denial took him through the path of his destiny. If Abraham had behaved greedily like Lot, he would not have fulfilled God's destiny for himself (Gen. 13:1-18; Acts 7:5).

The mystery of the power of choice is that while we are permitted or granted this power by God, our choices must be in Him or in obedience to His will. The Bible asserts that, he who finds a wife finds what is good and receives favor from the Lord (Prov. 18:22). Stressing the two sides of this verse, we can understand that though man does the finding or choosing, such a choice must be in line with God's desire. Our choice must not contradict or displease God; it must be of His delight. Of Israel He rebuked that they "...choose that in which I (God) delighted not" (Isa. 66:4 with emphasis).

To this end, we can now consider the basic or necessary ingredients of godly choice as it pertains to destiny, which would also leave pointers along the way on how to discover destiny. Note that destinies may look alike or fall into the same broad categories, yet there is always a difference. Just as you can never have two persons who are exactly the same, so also we can never have a similar destiny. Those who duplicate or copy others' destinies are those who have not really known how to identify their own destinies. A discovered or identified destiny is devoid of *me-tooism* or copycat syndrome. There may be challenges, of course. Destiny can also be collective (national destiny, for example) or individualistic. Whichever class it falls into, it remains unique.

THE INGREDIENTS OF GODLY CHOICE AND DISCOVERY OF DESTINY

1. Prayer:

The factors, as earlier mentioned, that may influence our choices negatively are very strong weapons of the devil, which can be overcome by prayer. When Jesus Christ was confronted by options of differing wills in Gethsemane, He prayed hard. In prayers, we speak and present to God our options and even our confusion. In the face of conflicting challenges of options, we can only go to our place of Gethsemane in prayer. Thus, it is only when we speak to God that we expect to hear from Him. Indeed, prayer is a key that unlocks the heavenly voice and revelation. God will always give us the right direction of choice that is in agreement with our destinies.

2. Fasting:

Through fasting, we can be better positioned spiritually to listen and hear from God. While prayer will help us to speak to God, fasting sharpens our sensitivity to hear from Him. Hence, our hearing from God will provide us with divine guidance, refocus our choices, and also reveal our destinies to us (Acts 13:2).

3. Counselling:

Often times, when we have prayed and God has spoken in return, we tend to only understand partially or not at all. In such situations, we need to seek for counseling, advice, or explanation. This is where many miss it. A clear definition of God's voice is important whenever He speaks to us. We must hear and also understand. In addition to going to Him in prayer to seek for direction, we should also seek His counsel. This is where the Bible, pastors, and parents become very important. The Bible says, "in the multitude of counselors there is safety" (Prov. 11:14).

We may not have only read or understood the Bible on certain issues, but we must also hear and receive understanding from those who have read the same thing. We might have read it with little or no understanding of what it means, but then those who have better understanding and experience can be reached out to for understanding.

Often times when destiny is not even understood, one can seek for pastoral counseling. A pastor is like a spiritual father. By taking sincere interest in you, he may, by revelation, have an understanding of your destiny as your spiritual father. When Samuel heard the voice of God and could not understand, he went to Eli for explanation, who carefully and properly guided him (1 Sam. 3: 1-10). In the same way, parents may sometimes provide insight and understanding that will guide our destiny. It is advisable to take time to listen to their wisdom and counsel, if they are walking in obedience to the Lord. When we humble ourselves before them, they can be of great help as far as destiny is concerned. Of course, that doesn't mean we are adjudicating the ability to make important life decisions to them, but having been involved in conceiving, birthing, and raising us from babyhood to adulthood, they must know a thing or two about our abilities, inclinations, and destiny. So, it makes sense that they might have some crucial inputs to make concerning our choices in particular and destinies in general, which must never be neglected.

Parents on their own must take serious the destinies of their children. There are certain things God reveals to parents that He expects to be passed on to the children. Destinies are often made known to parents. They must work toward it in the lives of their children while they are still living with them. They must also not hesitate to make inputs thereafter when they are on their own.

The destiny of Samson was revealed to his mother, and she took seriously the message conveyed by the visiting angel concerning Samson, along with her husband (Judg. 13:1- 25). It is entirely conceivable to me that the parents of Samson would not only have raised him in line with the message of his destiny they received through the angel, but would have also narrated the same to Samson as he was growing up.

The destiny of John the Baptist was also revealed to his parents, and they worked toward it (Lk. 1:13). Even when the process was about to be distorted in an attempt by the natives to give him a name that was not in harmony with his destiny (Lk. 1:13, 57-63), a name that would have been different from the name pronounced over him by the angel, his parents resisted it. Our names must be in accordance to our destiny. Similarly, I believe that John's parents would have also educated him regarding his destiny.

Regarding Jesus Christ, an angel of God revealed to His parents all about His destiny on earth (Matt. 1:18-21). Having been given the privilege of knowing His destiny, they worked toward its fulfillment and preservation even in the face of difficulty or pressure. For example, when, unknown to them, He stayed back in the temple, they went in desperate search for Him until they found him after three days (Lk. 2:41-51). From all indications, it's quite glaring that they would have educated Jesus generally on His destiny. We can also agree that He knew this from the Father in heaven as well. As we grow in obedience to God, we tend to realize that God still speaks and reveals destinies in different ways.

In those days in ancient Israel, the cool hours of the evening, after intense farm work in the scorching sun, provided moments for the family to gather for rest and for inspiring tales. The children would sit after dinner at the feet of the elders or parents for comical stories, ancestral narratives, or deliberations that may directly or indirectly revolve around their destinies.

Of course, in contemporary times, many parents leave the home before the children are awake from sleep and only breeze in while they've long gone to bed. We need to recover those precious moments with the kids for fellowship and destiny-shaping storytelling. Even at school, we should continue to encourage the efforts of godly guidance and counselling staff members who aid students in decision making - socially, morally, and otherwise - as it affects their choices in life and, consequently, their destinies. Christian counselling should continue to be an essential part of ministry. I know that some pastors are increasingly seeing individual counselling as something to be delegated away to others, but let's remember that we have been given the highest privilege to walk alongside others and help shape their destiny even in their vulnerable moments. Viewed that way, Christian counseling can become an important part of the discipleship process.

4. Patience:

One of the greatest enemies of a right choice is human hastiness. In patience, we learn to make the right choice. Impatience is a principal impediment to fulfilling destiny. In waiting on the Lord, we exercise a great deal of patience (Ps. 37:7; 40:1). Fulfilling destiny demands a great deal of patience. Patience is indeed one of the virtues of God Himself (Rom. 15:5). Destiny must be pursued with patience (Heb. 12:1). Every person has need of it, if we want to make the right choice and fulfill destiny. It's a fruit we must bear (Gal. 5:22).

5. Prayerful Declaration:

Father, I denounce today any choice I have made in life that will frustrate the fulfillment of my destiny. In Jesus' name. *Amen.*

THE TRANSITIONAL NATURE OF DESTINY

The most sensitive and systematic aspect of destiny is its transitional nature. Transition is the process and period of changing from one state or condition to another. The transitional nature of destiny has to do with its unfolding processes. Destiny is revealed or made known in a progressive or graduating approach.

Destiny unfolds over time, through developments and natural growth or progression. This unfolding nature is one aspect of divinity that does not make the things of God look abstract and magical. Divine things are clear and systematical processes, even when viewed spiritually from a natural perspective. The mystery and uniqueness of destiny is in God's wisdom of declaring the end from the beginning (Isa. 46:10). Truly, destiny is the platform of every prophetic insight to life. Prophetic release is drawn from destiny. While destiny has to do with future, prophecy is a statement that tells what will happen in the future. The two are never in conflict. Therefore, prophetic word cannot be outside destiny.

Those who understand and walk in the path of their destinies are likely to key into the prophetic realm; they enjoy the benefit of prophetic release. It readily works in them. The prophecies made about Timothy were on the basis of his destiny in regards to the calling of God upon him from the foundational and generational account of his mother and grandmother's sincere faith in God's prophecies (1 Tim. 1:18, 2 Tim. 1:5).

Let's critically examine again the mystery and uniqueness of destiny in the light of Genesis 1:26-28, which reveals that a man's creation is planned before it comes to pass. Now, we must understand that, at birth, it is not a man who is born but a baby. It then grows to a child and then to a man. However, God sees a man through to his completion, so what He sees is a man, even at birth. Note that destiny is the future man who has been earlier planned or decided upon in advance. This is the whole mystery of declaring the end from the beginning.

Thus, destiny unfolds in this categorical human symbolic order of nature: babyhood, childhood, and manhood. It follows that the path of destiny can be broken into these three developmental classes: nursing, training, and commission. Man goes through these different human developmental stages in life to become the destined man. Every man must be conscious of this. There is a time to be nursed, a time to be trained, and a time to be commissioned. The problem with many in fulfilling destiny is that they live and die as babies without ever transitioning (this is not a matter of calendar age or timing).

When they are supposed to pass through training or commissioning, they are still being nursed (Heb. 5:12), or when they are supposed to be commissioned, they are still undergoing training. Paul, at the time he was with Ananias and then taken to

Jerusalem, was to be introduced to the apostles by Barnabas (being nursed). Then, he was also taken by Barnabas to Antioch for the work of God and there, in Antioch, the training was possibly perfected, and he was consequently commissioned (Acts 9:10-18, 27; 11:25-26; 13:1-2).

This is emphasized in the life of Jesus Christ on earth and made more emphatic by the historic emphasis of place, time, and season in His life, in relevance to the transitional nature of His destiny. He was born in Bethlehem, raised in Nazareth, and began his ministry in Galilee. These locational or geographical factors in the unfolding process of Christ's destiny must be spiritually interpreted and absorbed. While Bethlehem was relatively a remote place, Nazareth was comparatively a town and, of course, Galilee was supposedly a city. They are arranged in His life in a progressive order of size and value. He began small and became big. The problem of man is that he desires to be big from the very start. Oftentimes, people want to be good leaders without necessarily being good followers. But to be able to be a great leader, one must first be a good follower.

Though you are called for a purpose, you have to pass through developmental stages to finally become or fulfill what you are destined for.

Jesus Christ could not have been born in Galilee and then began His ministry in Bethlehem as men would want to. That would have been contrary to the principle of divine order of transition. Nathaniel, like many today, misconstrued this divine order of transition. He demonstrates this through his doubt and objection to the reality of good things coming out of Nazareth. To him, if anything good could come, it would have to be from Galilee – a big place. This is ironic. In God's revelational way of doing things, He makes the small to bring today what may become big tomorrow, that way it can only take a divine revelation insight to discover His works. Of course, whatever that is of God can only be grasped by revelation.

Nathaniel, obviously manifested the lay spirit of his forefathers or what I call Israel's lay perception of Christ, many of whom will not adequately accept the messiahship of Jesus Christ on the basis of His humble birth. They are still expecting one who will come with a silver spoon.

There are many who are, at the moment, wanting to start in their Galilee. For God's destiny to be fulfilled in their lives, though, they must go back to their Bethlehem first. No more, no less. The more effective a baby crawls, the stronger it will walk.

But a baby that refuses to crawl and suddenly begins to walk has a likelihood to fall and be forced back by nature to crawl with the unstable or feeble feet that were unnecessarily hastened or unduly made to walk. This is what happens sometimes when we are suddenly made by God to experience again certain backward situations in life stages.

No stage must be skipped. Often, we may want to skip Nazareth (childhood), the training time, because it is the most critical time, even though it is mainly a sowing and laboring time alone. But, all it needs is obedience, humility, submission, commitment, patience, focus, and endurance to become a time we see with eyes of excitement and expectation.

TWO BROAD PRINCIPLE PERSPECTIVES OF THE TRANSITIONAL NATURE OF DESTINY

1.The two-fold extreme principles of the transitional nature of destiny:

These are the "beginning" and the "end" principles Ecclesiastes 7:8 and Isaiah 46:10. Solomon was a man who experienced a rather better end than beginning, while Isaiah relatively encountered a better beginning than end. These patterns informed their views on this two-fold extreme.

Now, destiny is caged in two integral extremes. Every man that must get to the end of a matter or task he embarks upon in life must often have a formidable beginning (Prov. 20:2; Ecc. 3:11). These are two-fold points of destiny. Thus, without a firm beginning, the end is most likely in vain. Men are full of tasks that have no trace of beginning, sometimes having a great work that bears little or no beginning, a mere shallow take off.

Every success that is not a product of the unfolding process of destiny will someday suffer an abrupt collapse. It will never get to its destination. Every destiny that goes in this principle order of transition will become a sort of success that begins and ends in failure or collapse. The take-off or the beginning may be challenging, but what we mainly need are boldness, firmness, and obedience, etc. With these, irrespective of the satanic plots, destiny will surely be fulfilled.

There can be some satanic organized distractions but remain focused. Center on the major. Never allow lesser purpose to deny you greater purpose. Know that good can be the enemy of the best. Be conscious of growth and progression in fulfilling destiny.

As we grow in life, whatever task or learning God permits us to begin or be involved in will have a way of contributing to what we will ultimately do and end or become in life. No time must be wasted in tasks that will not be part or relevant to what we shall ultimately settle for in regards to destiny. If there is time devoted to such tasks, they will result in the deflection of destiny. Of course, there can be rare exceptions. While we may be involved in several other fields or functions in life, we must prioritize our core mission. How can one who wants to be a seamstress in life begin and spend long years in learning to bake and only to go back to the former, or one who is destined to be a politician spend years studying medicine? It's a deviation of destiny, indeed. Destiny is not a game of chance. Adhesion is important. While those who stick to a specific endeavor over time are always stable and better in life, those who waver and falter about will always experience crawling or faltering in life.

We must spend our strength on tasks which align with our destiny. We must strive to stay and be known for specific life endeavors and create a legacy even after our exit on earth. One of the frustrating effects against destiny is reflected in the logical attitude of the "jack of all trade and master of none syndrome". There are many who are full of activities and yet no specific area of specialization, no steady adhesion and identifiable responsibility exists. This will certainly end in an unfulfilled destiny. It is better to be known in a little task than to stay among many great tasks. This is what has become of many destinies today. God will surely help us.

2. The seed principles of the transitional nature of destiny:

This principle is threefold: Fall, Die, and Bear (or Bring)

"...Except a corn of wheat (seed) 'fall' into the ground and 'die', it abideth alone; but if it die, it 'bringeth' forth much fruit" (Jn. 12:24 [emphasis added])

The seed will first fall into the ground, then it dies, and finally, it begins to bear or bring fruits. In this order, human destiny also goes through transition. Jesus Christ used the corn of wheat symbolically of Himself, even as it applies to all men, signifying that to fall into the ground and then die will precede fruitfulness and abundance. The former are expressive of His cross experience and to us a time of great humility. This three-fold order in John 12:24 is, in Ephesians 4:9-10, further reduced to a twofold encompassing period: dissension and ascension.

"Now that He ascended, what is it but that he also descended first into the lower parts of the earth? He that descended is the same also that ascended up far above all heavens, that he might fill all things?" (Eph. 4:9-10).

Paul, by the Holy Spirit, stresses here that Christ first descended before ascending, not the contrary. We must not ascend to descend but, rather, descend to ascend. It's down, then up. Christ was destined a "King" - at birth, He was prophetically declared a Savior and King by the gospels of Luke and Matthew, respectively (Lk. 2:11; Matt. 2:2). Nevertheless, the Bible says He took the form of a servant (not king), transitioning from a lamb to sheep and then to a shepherd. Examine this logical trend of growth, for there lies the mystery of the unfolding process of destiny (the transitional nature of destiny). This cannot be broken. We have so many assumed shepherds who first were neither lamb nor sheep. It can't work. It will only end in frustration sooner than later.

The further we go in the process, the harder it seems, yet we get closer and closer to the crown and the joy of destiny fulfilled. The closer the dawn, the darker the sky becomes (Heb. 12:1-3).

This is revealed in Proverbs 4:18. The further our destiny is advanced, the more it seems the challenge is on the one side, and on the other, the more accomplished or fruitful we abound or it becomes.

The path of destiny must be followed. Those who failed surely failed because the path of fulfilling destiny was not followed. Barak Obama did not become the first black President of the United States just because he was destined but because he followed the path of fulfilling destiny. We can be destined to be great and yet, without adhering to the principles of the transitional stages of destiny, it can never be fulfilled. It will only amount to nothing.

Joseph's destiny was convincingly revealed that he was to be great. Yet, in fulfilling it, he kept and followed the road to becoming great. It's sweat to sweet; pit and prison to palace. We are first enclosed or isolated from outside influence and contact before we are disclosed; the place of power is in the former. Power is received in the enclosure of the upper room or indoor and not in the disclosure of the public or outdoor. Acts 10:38 says, "He went about (in public) doing good, and healing all who were possessed by the devil because God was with Him (in private)". In private or indoors, we receive from God, but in public or outdoors, we give to men.

DECREE:

Father, I receive the grace and wisdom to transit in the path of my destiny.

DESTINY FOR DESTINY

Destiny for destiny simply speaks to the synergy effect, or the combined effects of two or more destinies that exceeds the strength of their individual output and the principles of mutual dependency and co-existence, which does not undermine God's perfect work in man as an individual. The book of Genesis declares that it is not good for a man to be alone. This statement implies the concept of this subtopic. The phrase "not good" is, in context, referring to a destiny that is not in destiny, an isolated destiny. Adam was alone and needed to blend together with another destiny.

After the work of creation was completed, God declared in Genesis 1:31 that it was exceedingly good. God's words "not good", however, implies that man's destiny was less than ideal and, therefore, not complete without the woman's destiny. Destiny is complementary, like involving different modes of transportation to get to a destination. For instance, in the same way that travel modes are complementary—such as using a plane for long stretches, a ferry to get across a bay, or a car for closer drives within neighborhoods—destinies can be complementary to one another. This is a logical explanation of the concept and principle of destiny for destiny. Now, as strong, fast, and comfortable as the plane is, it can't drop its passengers at their ultimate destinations; it can't just go beyond the airport. The passenger needs the additional involvement of other vehicles. In the same way, many destinies, though great, are unable to experience fulfillment because they need integration with another destiny to stir them up for fulfillment.

No destiny can be fulfilled in isolation. The verb or phrase "help meet" in Genesis 2:18 basically means to aid or supply that which an individual cannot provide for himself. It implies an addition or complement and does not indicate inferiority or subordination. The woman is also made in the image of God and, therefore, is equal to man. Hence, no destiny is inferior to another. When destinies are integrated, none should be considered better or relegated. Naaman's great achievement was never more valuable than the value of the idea or information the little maid in his house provided. A product that is needed by more than a man needs more than one man's destiny to be produced. A destiny can be for a man but must be fulfilled along and among other destinies. God does not put everything completely in one destiny; He created others so that He could make complete what is needed in another destiny. Destinies must be augmented. It is the will and desire of God to destinies to co-exist or come together for effect. It is not based on inadequacies or limitations, per se. It is based on principle. This is demonstrated by the use of the plural pronoun "us" in the biblical account of the creation of man. God the Father alone could have been able to do the work of human creation as well, but there was a functional integration of the Godhead. This principle is not limited to the creation of man. He further expects that the same principle is applied in our fulfilling destiny. Destinies must be blended together for their ultimate fulfillment. Integration with relevant destinies must not be induced by emotion or sentiment. Any time God aligns destinies together, there is always a defined aim or purpose in fulfilling the destiny at stake.

Sometimes, you can recognize your need for destiny integration when you are full of ideas but lack the ability to actualize a full vision or project by yourself. Being unable to go at it alone is not a sign of weakness; it is a call, a reason, to align one destiny to another. Destiny is a force that can draw men together. Every God-given opportunity to mesh destinies must be taken seriously and conscientiously. Truly, the destiny of one man can help shape up another man's own destiny. Just as a nation can greatly help build another nation's destiny. The United States government, at certain times, is considered wasteful in expending heavy resources to defend other smaller nations' interests and challenges, yet some of these nations in question may, consequently, come out someday strong. America infused its destiny into Kuwait when Iraq invaded her. That singular integration of destiny by the U.S. might have preserved and strengthened the destiny of Kuwait and, for this purpose, nations view seriously a bilateral or multilateral agreement or treaty with other nations. Colonialism, I strongly believe, is God's intent arrangement for stronger nations to help build other weak nations at a given time. Through colonial power, dependent nations and their economies have grown to become independent. This may not come all that easily because there is always the human factor and satanic manipulations. Oppression and exploitations can set in to fight God's original purpose, thereby portraying this heavenly plan as slavery and bondage.

While it's necessary for "destiny in destiny" to occur, integrating one's destiny in a wrong destiny will yield nothing. It will amount to a square peg in a round hole. We must trust and commit this to God, as there is always a divinely appointed partner to the fulfillment of every destiny. Abraham and Hagar constituted a square peg in a round hole, for through Abraham and Hagar came Ishmael and never Isaac the promised one. Only Abraham and Sarah were able to bring the latter. We can have results without fulfillment. As long as Ishmael is the result, there can never be fulfillment. There are so many efforts that are merely yielding Ishmaels, due to improper blending of destinies.

When destinies are heavenly infused, none should be relegated or despised. The captive Israelite girl who served Naaman's wife became an important and fundamental instrument in the healing of the dreaded and disgraceful leprosy of the great but proud Naaman. As relegated and neglected as some people may seem to be in our lives, God may well use them for our major breakthrough. While this little maid's impact in the house of Naaman might have, before then, been considered relatively insignificant, her destiny, blended with Naaman's, led to his healing. Despite all the achievements of Naaman, it took the idea or information of this little maid to bring fulfillment to him. Sometimes, great things are packaged or disguised in things or persons that we may not humanly see or esteem. Such was the case of this little maid.

PURPOSE OF DESTINY FOR DESTINY

Great blessing are embedded in the synergy of destiny for destiny. These will include eight major factors. It is worthy to note that Christ had, on Earth, infused His destiny into that of His apostles. This can be affirmed by scriptural accounts of the lives of the apostles at the exit of Christ on earth.

1. For procreation and productive synergy:

The blending of Adam and Eve was for this purpose. It's for propagative purposes and for a more productive strength. The first Adamic covenant has as one of its obligations, the responsibility of bearing and refiling the earth with humans: "And God blessed them, and God said unto them, be fruitful, and multiply, and replenish the earth…" (Gen. 1 :27).

This could not have been executed or fulfilled by man without the woman. The two destinies were infused together for this purpose (Gen. 2:28). God cannot break his principles. When destinies are divinely integrated, it results in synergy; for two are better than one because they have a good return for their work. One shall chase a thousand and two will put ten thousand to flight. And, if one falls down, his friend can help him up (Ecc. 4:9-12; Matt 18:19-20). When Christ sent His disciples out, He sent them in twos, upholding this principle of destiny-for-destiny synergic viewpoint. Just look at the great exploits of the pairing effects of Peter and John, Paul and Barnabas, and Pricilla and Aquila—who, besides their procreative activities, were together a more productive strength in the work of the gospel. Every Christian couple or marriage must functionally be viewed in this way.

2. For a call:

God had arranged the infusing of the destiny of the young Samuel to that of Eli mainly for the purpose of pronouncing His call upon Samuel. One wonders how a man who could not raise his own children in the ways of the Lord and the priesthood would have the capacity to raise another's son in the capacity of a priest. The truth remains that God had destined Samuel to be called while with Eli, which may be the singular reason Eli had strength enough to complete this mission. Sometimes, a destiny is integrated into another destiny just to have a call pronounced. Eli indeed had guided Samuel in regards to the calling voice of God, which Samuel could not earlier understand, and that alone was great, for Eli no doubt knew that Samuel was going to be great, possibly greater than him. Even then, he did not frustrate or refuse to guide the young lad. Even if Samuel had not benefitted in any other way from Eli, Eli empowered him to hear the voice of the Lord. This may just be the reason destiny engaged with destiny.

3. For a collective commission:

The integration of the destinies of Barnabas and

Paul is an amazing demonstration of this factor. Paul, previously named Saul, was saved and went to Jerusalem to see and/or join himself with the apostle but was rejected, and Barnabas discretionally took him back to the apostles for acceptance. Thereafter, Paul again left for Tarsus, possibly due to discouragement. There are many converts who, because of discouragement, might have gone back to their Tarsus. Barnabas further went to Tarsus, picked up Paul, and together, they travelled to Antioch where they began to teach. The impact of this led the local people to call the disciples, perhaps for the first time, Christians. Now, it's no doubt that Paul would have been trained in teaching ministry there in Antioch. May we also be wise enough to go back to where our converts have been drawn back to and bring them back for edification and service. After this, the men were commissioned by the Holy Ghost (Acts 13:2).

Look at this amazing work of God in blending destinies. These two men were destined to do the work together. God integrated these destinies together for the common commissioning of both of them. God may have given someone to each of us for the purpose of being commissioned together. We must be careful with the men God has given to us. Imagine what could have happened if Barnabas had abandoned Paul. Our commission for certain vial tasks in life may just be waiting for our raising of that fellow God has infused our destiny into. The man Barnabas must be recommended. I wish for us all to have the spirit of Barnabas today, a spirit which does not shy from apostolic grace in any arena. It is also of note that men must be of careful the way they leave their trainers or place of training, as some are destined to humbly stay and serve with the same trainer or remain in the same place of training, temporarily or permanently.

4. For succession:

Destiny can be in destiny for succession's sake. A classic example is that of Elijah and Elisha. There was no clear scriptural evidence that Elijah actually trained Elisha, compared to the experience and account of Barnabas and Paul. The emphasis in Elijah's story was more on succession; somebody was to succeed Elijah and that was Elisha's destiny. I have always believed that Elisha followed Elijah not only to learn but for the purpose of receiving that mantle. Like Barnabas, Elijah knew Elisha was his successor and was possibly going to, by the grace of God, overshadow Elijah in history. In fact, Elijah specifically asked Elisha for a double portion of his anointing. This request could not have been for any other desire than to sincerely do better than his master. Anointing is the practical effect and demonstration of grace, and we are given grace according to the measure of the gift or ability of God upon us. The bible further says, He gave them talents according to their individual abilities. Thus, our ability is a function of the anointing of God upon us. Hence, Elisha was telling his master that he hoped to be even greater than him. Elijah understood all this and yet he was not envious. Jesus Christ Himself emphatically declared that His disciples would do greater works than He had done on Earth. Can we stand the presence of a younger person or follower who would have the grace to do better than us when we're out of the scene? Elisha saw the end of his master when he was taken from him. We must be ready to take along anyone who is truly destined and willing to the very point of our handing over to Him our own mantles.

True succession has become difficult today, both physically and spiritually, because destinies are not integrated together for this purpose. It is either frustrated or aborted to this effect, and we keep recycling leaders. What do you say of a man in his seventies aspiring to become a minister in a government of a nation where there are surplus of great potentials amongst the young men? Amazingly, the same man had served in the same capacity in three past generations of leadership in the country.

If God has integrated a man's destiny into another for the purpose of succession, oftentimes persecution and trials may come. Despite this, one must not be deterred. David was highly persecuted by Saul, whom he was to succeed. He was chased around like rat by the king, and yet David never gave up. He never took vengeance or ran away. He knew it was a matter of time before he would step in and take up the throne of leadership. In the face of all this, David still infused his destiny into that of Saul. It was not broken. Our predecessor may know God's succession plan for us, and may even be used by the devil to frustrate it by any means whatsoever. Don't give up or run away. Just remain courageous and obedient while counting it as part of the transitional experience and training to get to the top. Be wise.

5. For riches and protection:

Sometimes, when God wants to richly establish

someone who seems humanly helpless, He simply will attach or integrate such a destiny into another privileged one. Such was the situation of Lot with Abraham, for Lot neither had a father nor a mother. God permitted the integration of his destiny into Abraham's for his ultimate prosperity and protection through Abraham. The wealth of Abraham enhanced him and, by extension, he became rich. Even if orphaned, God has a way of integrating our destinies into others for the purpose of being helped.

Apart from making Lot rich, Abraham went further to protect him and fought for him against his arch enemies. Abraham released his destiny into that of Lot, knowing that doing so would prosper and shield Lot.

There are people who God has designed to fuse their destinies with ours in order that we can provide for them. We must not fail. We must work hard, accept and fulfill it, irrespective of their shortfalls or weakness or ingratitude. Though Lot never encouraged Abraham in return for his good will toward him, Abraham continued in his good deeds. It's about God and not man. Consequently, God blessed Abraham soon after Lot left. So many people have failed in this obligation. Some would only wish they are given another opportunity to help. God knows all. This must not be our portion.

6. For conversion and demonstration of His glory:

One might wonder why God would have permitted young Hebrew believers like Daniel and his cohorts to be taken captive by a wicked and unbelieving king and kingdom. God can permit the destiny of a believer to be blended into that of an unbeliever—possibly in service, business, marriage, etc.—for the purpose of converting the latter. This is not an encouragement for a believer to go into marriage with an unbeliever. The point here is that God can do exceptional things at His discretion. The destinies of these Hebrew boys were, by God, integrated into the destiny of the strange king and kingdom for the purpose of demonstrating His glory and power and bring the fear of the true God upon them. This they no doubt performed. It was on this same principle that God instructed Hosea, the prophet, to again get married to Gomer, the prostitute. It was for the demonstration of His mercy and salvation of Israel.

Such is never a time to be carried away and become like nonbelievers. The Hebrew boys resisted; we can, as well, resist every temptation. Any time God (not man) integrates destinies of such two extremes it must be seen as a reason to make converts and demonstrate His power and glory through us to them. Only men of great grace will He use in this direction. May we not fail Him. Joseph never failed God at any point in fulfilling destiny. He had his destiny severely infused into unbelievers. Remember, by integrating the destiny of Joseph into that of Pharaoh in Egypt, not only was the nation of Egypt saved from famine, Joseph's family found help in a period of a severe famine. Joseph overcame temptations and excelled in the house of Potiphar by refusing to give in to the antics and pressures of his master's wife. There, in Egypt, in the house of Pharaoh, he distinguished himself as one that feared the Lord. The major challenge of the church today is having believers who can translate God's kingdom power practically into the kingdom of the world, who can overcome the likes of Potipher's lustful and manipulative wife and keep integrity in the governance and administration of their Egypt. We need the Daniels that can stand their own in the midst of the enticing delicacies of the palace and the direct threat to compromise their faith by forces and agents of darkness. Until our minds are transformed concerning this, we may never raise leaders in the fold.

DECREE:

Father, I integrate my destiny into destinies that are for the good of my fulfilling destiny.

CONCLUSION

Destiny is two sided. God is the originator of our destinies. He made and makes us to conform to our various destinies. On the other side, it's left for us humans to choose correctly and align and adapt the progressive stages of destiny and, of course, have our destinies integrated into other God-designed relevant destinies for the fulfillment of our own destinies.

There is never a conflict between our God-given destinies and His works in us. On the side of God, we are indeed an exact product of our destinies. We are originally made entirely capable of fulfilling destiny. God ever remains able. As the physical child is never in doubt over his father's ability to provide and protect him, so also in the spiritual, the believer must believe that God is ever able. We must see ourselves as the problem that can still be changed by God to conform to our destinies. As God never changes, so do our destinies never change (Heb. 1:12; 13:8). Doing the right thing on our side will surely bring our destinies. God is able to keep his own commitment. Knowingly or unknowingly, by our actions and utterances, we tend to shift blames on God when our destinies are under attack. Let's repent of this and, with our whole heart, believe God. He never breaks His covenant (Ps. 89:34). Destiny is real. You will surely fulfill your destiny. Amen.

Instead of the desperation for prophecies, which many are falsely using to lure, manipulate and take undue advantage of the ignorant ones, people should take time to understand their destinies. It is because of this lack of understanding that there is this desperation for prophesy and deliverance. Some of the experiences we go through in life are mainly to move us to the next level of life, not to destroy us. We can only know if we understand our destinies. Joseph's chains of bitter experiences were made to enhance the fulfillment of his destiny. Today, that may be misinterpreted to mean ancestral or generational curses or demonic oppression and possession, which could frustrate the will of God. If no one attacked or crucified Christ, the work of our redemption would not have been achieved. Sometimes, God permits our afflictions for our own good (1 Cor. 2:8). The devil's attacks against us are often times a disadvantage to his own self, while also an advantage to us (Phil. 1:28).

PART TWO
INTRODUCTION

"Fulfilling Destiny" is aimed at expatiating the concept of destiny. The emphasis on this subject matter is due to the fact that it's one area where many struggle. One's divine understanding of destiny fulfillment propels them to keep pushing forward, even in the face of challenges or obstacles. This section is no doubt a blue print for destiny and its fulfillment.

Fulfilling destiny is every man's ultimate goal on earth. Man is a product of destiny, which is fulfilled when we have accomplished in life on earth God's plan for us, having been divinely planned before our birth (Jer. 1:4-10; Isa. 49:1-5, Gal. 1:15-20; Exo. 33:12-13). Destiny is the power believed to control events of life (Gen. 1:26-27). Hence, life's events are centered on one's destiny, irrespective of the way and manner they unfold. Destiny differs from purpose. While destiny involves the entire makeup of life, purpose is just a narrow segment of destiny. The former involves one's nature, personality, purpose and goal.

Every man has a unique and uncommon destiny.

Destiny fulfillment can include activities or events in life unfolding in manners that are not humanly understandable, unless one is in tune or in relationship with God. This is simply because destiny is absolutely of God and, therefore, takes Him to comprehend this essential mystery of life.

Now, destiny must be handled in the same way the eagle handles its movement in the air. Eagles soar. There isn't any struggle–it yields to the directional dictates of the stormy nature in the atmosphere. We must, in like manner, yield our life to destiny in God.

Obviously, when life and the Bible are not interpreted based on a clear understanding of destiny, it will result in wrong and complex interpretations and, consequently, wrong applications. This is the reason many have always misinterpreted the book of Ruth. The book is a typical analysis of destiny and how it's fulfilled. The book of Ruth is a complete and profound record and study of the fulfillment of the destiny of Ruth. Indeed, all other characters or personalities major or minor are merely destinies God had blended into Ruth's destiny principally for her own fulfillment of destiny.

To this effect, it's my strong belief that anyone that reads and opens their heart to the wonderful work of God in this book will ever appreciate God's human creation as it pertains to destiny. Ruth's destiny fulfillment occurred in such a way that no man could humanly figure beforehand how it would end up. This is typical of how every destiny would be fulfilled.

I trust God that as you read on, you will suddenly comprehend and discover why sometimes things were or are so with you, and with this understanding, we can now remain firm without giving up in whatever situations and circumstances of life. We will surely fulfill our destinies. Ruth did, and we can't be an exception. "God is the same yesterday, and today and forever" (Heb. 13:8).

The second half of this book is broken into the following sections: Your Naomi, Trials of life, Your Boaz, The place of wisdom, The place of humility, The place of favor, and Providence.

Finally, I wish to humbly admonish that you quickly reread the book of Ruth before the commencement of this study. This is not just because the study is drawn from the book but also because it will enhance assimilation and application of the revelational benefits of this book. It must further be understood that though the book of Ruth is not a direct spiritual context, it is meant by God to simply portray the natural phenomenon of certain spiritual truths and realities, using the earthly (visible) to explain the spiritual (invisible) (Rom. 1:20; Jn. 3:12). Ruth stands symbolic of a child of God, while Boaz stands symbolic of God.

-Stewart MBA

YOUR NAOMI

It all began in the days when the judges ruled Israel (Ruth 1:1). It was indeed a temporary period of rulership, a militaristic regime transitioning to civil rule. This was by God's arrangement. We must always hope that God will someday change our terrible situations to His desired will for us. We must have faith and patience (2 Cor. 4:17). It will surely come to pass that if we follow with faith and patience, we will inherit the promise (Heb. 6:12).

Israel was in the wrong when they demanded God to grant them kings instead of judges (1 Sam. 8). It was outside His will. However, He can always allow things to happen, even if they are outside His will. God desired a king as well, just not in the timing the Israelites were asking for. It is one thing to have God's will granted to us at our own time; it is another thing to have it when it's His own time for it. We must not only go for God's promises or desires for us, we must as well conform and confine it to His timing for us; unless it's on God's perfect will, fulfillment remains elusive. This was the case with Israel. We must always make sure that we've patiently met God's requirement before our requests or prayers. This is because petitions can be answered based on either the permissive or the perfect will of God, implying that when we pray without meeting God's requirement or obedience, He may just answer us according to His permissive will. This must not be an ultimate desire of His children.

Now, the Judges' period was short. Meanwhile, a king was divinely in the making, as God was preparing a great king for Israel (1 Sam. 16:1). God was yet bent on fulfilling His will. He will always perfect His will. Our present situation notwithstanding, God's ultimate plan for us is in progress and undistorted.

Thus, Naomi divinely became God's instrument of righteousness (Rom. 1:13) in the whole process of locating and raising God's choice king for Israel and, ultimately, the king for all of humanity. Ruth bore a son who became the grandfather of Judah's greatest king: David. Realize, though, that Ruth could not bear a child for Chilion, her late husband, as that was not the destined pairing.

Now, Naomi, Elimelech her husband, and two sons: Mahlon and Chilion had to leave their land, Bethlehem, to a less honorable land called Moab, a Gentile nation for succor. There, a special lady called Ruth would be found. This can in no ways be comprehended humanly; it's a mystery of life, a divine truth of real life that is beyond human reasoning. Thus, the discovery of Ruth all began. She married one of Naomi's sons. There are those who should do the locating, and there are others who are to be located. Indeed, there are those whose task is to discover gifts and also there are those whose work is to prepare the way for others. Some of us may, at certain times, not be leaders but are very important instruments in determining who leads. These are both essential roles. We must know where we belong in each time and situation.

Truly, at any time God is in need of us in another location or task for a divine assignment or purpose, He does all to move us; such was the case of Naomi. Hence, God allowed famine in Naomi's Bethlehem so as to compel them to move. Just like the young eagles, when it's time for them to leave the confinement of their nest and fend for themselves, as well experience a soaring life of maturity in the storm, the mother eagle goes to the extent of intentionally dismantling the nest—their comfort zone— to compel them to vacate the nest for a new life. There is always a God-allowed famine in our self-desired habitation in order to move us. Oftentimes, the storms we face at a given place, time, or situation implies that it's time to adjust or move, and that we are not or no longer in the place of destiny. This does not mean that we should keep changing locations. It's a matter of deep spiritual connotation. We must be where God wants us to be. It's not a physical thing. Not all storms are actually meant for our destruction. For instance, the storm of Jonah came because he was in a place of disobedience. He remained in the wrong place and time. That storm cannot stop until there is an obedient change to the right place. It is associated with disobedience.

Other storms are mere phenomenal attempts by the devil against the obedient children of God in this life. Hence, it can be stopped after it's divinely rebuked, for in this, Christ is always available to calm.

Remember, God is not found in a place where we stubbornly choose to be. Jonah's storm is what every man that lives in disobedience of any form is bound to experience. It is not for me to say that Naomi and her household travelling to Moab to avoid the famine was wrong. Such judgements would only amount to judging a matter with just a part of the truths and would demonstrate a lack of understanding of the mystery of destiny. When we understand the mystery of destiny, certain divinely induced decisions of men, no matter how wrong it may look in the eyes of man, may just be geared toward fulfilling destiny.

Never make a judgement based strictly on the beginning of a matter without the end. The Bible affirms that though the beginning declares the end, yet greater is the end of a matter than the beginning (Isa. 46:10; Ecc. 7:8). By the revelation of the concluding part of the Book of Ruth, we should agree that the famine and all of Naomi's losses were allowed by God for a purpose, so Ruth's destiny could be fulfilled.

I declare to you today, that God will, to your Naomi, allow a famine in their Bethlehem until they leave to look for you. Such was the case of Naomi concerning Ruth. This may just be what your gifts needs. Remember that it was in like manner that the whole Earth then suffered famine, except Egypt where Joseph would be found by his brothers (Gen. 41:57; 42:1-32, 45, and 46). The famine in Bethlehem was to locate Ruth in Moab.

Naomi's two sons married Orphah and Ruth in Moab. Now, understand that after these two ladies came into their new family, something terrible happened. Naomi was stripped of all her possessions (Ruth 1:21). You may wonder why. It's simple; whenever we locate the desire of God, He strips us of all our own desires. Ruth was located, which was followed by Naomi losing her husband and both her sons. Discovering Ruth was almost reflective of Christ's parables of the hidden treasures and of the pearl of great price which, when they were found, were exchanged for all that the founder had. The Bible says that when the man had found the hidden treasure in a field, he hid it and went and sold all that he had in exchange for the field. Notice that it's not in exchange for the pearl but for the field. In other words, he directly went for the source, which was wise and thoughtful of him (Matt. 13:44-46). It is also important to note that the man, after he had found the hidden treasure, re-hid it, this time from others until he had sold all he had in order to acquire it.

What this implies is that he never exposed or put to use what he had not paid for nor justified keeping it. This is the area where we easily fail. It's great lesson for us. What it means is that until we have paid the price for what God is doing (or, at least, are assured that His favor is upon us), we many have no need to make it public. We might have found grace, yet we must wait patiently in training and service to pay the price for our gift before we make it known to others. Gifts and ministries have gone down not because they lacked grace but for the unpaid syndrome status situation (SSS).

Ruth was, indeed, like the hidden treasure in the field or the precious pearl, and Naomi's husband and two sons were like the price Naomi paid in exchange for Ruth. But Ruth became more valuable to Naomi than seven sons (Ruth 4:15).

It was after Ruth was discovered that the famine in Bethlehem was over. It follows, therefore, that it's when we have accomplished a certain will of God that He makes the associated famine in our life end. Thus, it was time for the women to return to the place of destiny fulfillment. There is always a place and time of destiny fulfillment. Christ's place of fulfillment was not Egypt but Jerusalem. Egypt was a mere hide out, a refuge, from the murderous and wicked King Herod, an enemy of the supreme destiny of Christ. Christ would never have fulfilled His destiny in Egypt. Therefore, Herod had to die according to God's will to give room for Jesus to come back to Jerusalem: His place of destiny fulfillment (Mt. 2:13-15,19).

So many of us are still in our Moab or Egypt, and there can never be destiny fulfillment out there. We must relocate or go back to our Jerusalem. Many destinies are struggling for fulfillment even with all the riches and strength available to them because they are still off from the place of their fulfillment. Jerusalem may just be spiritual adherence to our real calling or a good attitude toward God. It could also mean avenues or people whom God has prepared for us to help or to help us in fulfilling our destinies.

TRIALS OF LIFE

We all face trials of life in the fulfillment of destiny. Trials are as inevitable as destiny itself. Both cannot be aborted. While fulfillment may fail, destiny cannot. Fulfillment lies within man, while destiny is absolutely of God. If we permit the devil, he can and will abort, distort, or frustrate our destiny fulfillment. Our destinies ever remain intact. Nothing can ever destroy or change them. If we make the right choice, live in obedience to God, and patiently follow life's transitional process, then fulfillment becomes possible. Destiny is like a destination, and fulfilling it is like the road to a destination. The destination remains constant and stable, while the road can be missed and traced back again. To destroy a destiny is like uprooting a destination, which is not practically possible. So, destiny cannot be destroyed.

There will always be tests and trials in life. Before every stage of genuine progress and fulfillment in life, there is a corresponding phase of trial for the new level of promotion and destiny fulfillment. Each time hope comes in life, there also comes a seemingly hopeless situation for us to overcome. There is always a hopeless situation because there is first a hopeful situation. It is only when God opens a door for us that the devil fights to close it. The devil does not try to close a door that is already closed. It is only when hope comes that we are made to experience a time of opposition. This was exactly the experience of Paul at a certain time of his life and ministry. He writes, "because a great door for effective work was opened to me and there are many who oppose me" (1 Cor. 16:9).

We must not give up when we are faced with hopeless situations and oppositions. They are rather proofs or indications that there is hope ahead. In the same way, Ruth was brought to her place of destiny fulfillment, but not without some trials.

Trials here can be broken into two levels, namely: partial and total trials. Ruth experienced both of these. The partial trial came by way of "rejection with hospitality," while the total trial by way of "rejection with hostility".

For the nature of the partial trial, let's read: Ruth1: 8-10:

"Then Naomi said to her two daughters-in-law, Go back, each of you, to your mother's home. May the Lord show kindness to you, as you have shown to your dead and to me. May the Lord grant that each of you will find rest in the home of another husband. Then she kissed them and they wept aloud and said to her, we will go back with you to your people".

And for the nature of the total trial, let's read Ruth 1:11-14:

"But Naomi said, Return home, daughters. Why should you come with me? Am I going to have any more sons? At this, they wept again.

Then Orpah kissed her Mother – in – law good bye, but Ruth clung to her."

In the first trial, Naomi ordered the girls to go back pleasantly and even went further to bless them, kissing them all the way. In the second, she did not only order them to go but she stirred hopelessness in them as she vented her outright anger and regret on them. Both Orpah and Ruth were able to overcome the first trial, while only Ruth survived the second.

The analytical truth here is that if we must really fulfill our destinies on earth, then we must be ready to overcome both levels of trial. Oftentimes, we tend to like Orpah and survive our first trial but not the second. We must be ready and bold enough to surmount trials of absolute rejection, without compromising, even when there is no one to help or pamper us. We must have a firm commitment to faith in God.

We tend to only withstand partial trials and give in during the trials of outright rejection. Orpah overcame the first trial but could not withstand the second, leaving alone, of course, Ruth, the destined one. Yes, Ruth persisted and was resilient and steadfast (Ruth 1:18). In the face of extreme trials, those who exhibit courage and faith will certainly emerge victorious and praiseworthy. Persistency and steadfastness are the keys (1 Pt. 1:7-8).

Christ's ultimate trial of the redemption of man on the cross was an absolute or total rejection, as sorrowfully expressed by Christ Himself, "My God, My God, why have you forsaken me?" (Matt. 27:26). He, however, overcame and, consequently, His assignment on earth was perfected; He fulfilled His destiny (Jn. 19:30).

In like manner, we should remain steadfast in trials of any nature or level. We can, indeed! God has given us the capacity and ability in Christ Jesus for "no temptation has seized you except what is common to man. And God is faithful; he will not let you be tempted beyond what you can bear" (1 Cor. 10:13).

Truly, great blessings and fulfillment will always be preceded by great trials. James 1:12 says that those who persevere under trial will receive the crown of life that God has promised to those who love him. Believers must all understand that trials are not made to afflict, destroy, or fail us. It does not portray hatred of any kind. It's to ascertain our capacity and actually prepare us for the next level of life and destiny fulfillment. The strength of a given trial represents the measure and nature of expectation and challenge in a potential future or further stage of life. It's like a pre-experience. Hence, every level of progress in destiny fulfillment has its own gravity and nature of trial. The more we progress in our destiny fulfillment, the more complex the trials, the more the expectant higher level progress and, indeed, grace. God will never move us to a new or higher level until we are able to first overcome the corresponding trial prior to or meant for that level.

Obviously, when some trials come, we should be glad as long as we are living in obedience. It's an indication of a coming promotion. We must not compromise; like Ruth, we should not give up. We must face it. God is never done with us because we faced and failed a trial, but rather, He graciously gives us more time and opportunity to prepare again. It's for good because when we overcome trials and are then promoted, the devil and his cohorts will hardly bring us down again at that given stage of life, having been tested and proven. Those who shy away from trials invariably stay away from genuine or divine promotion indeed. This is what the Bible teaches. It's well. So don't give up.

We must be patient if destiny must be greatly fulfilled. Great things don't always manifest fast and easily. We are told of an Asian giant bamboo tree with a hard seed which needs to be watered and fertilized for four years consistently before it sprouts or any portion of it breaks the soil. However, in the fifth year, the tree shows itself and begins to grow at an average rate of four feet a day to a height of ninety feet in less than a month. It is believed that one can almost stand by it and watch it grow. This truly applies to life; people want to see quick manifestation. It must not always be so. Plant the seed in obedience, then wait patiently and continue to work hard.

It is important that we don't drift from our destiny and destiny fulfillment. Like the giant bamboo hard seed, the beginning may be slow but the latter end will increase greatly. We must not despise the period of waiting. We must not walk away from our destiny at any point in time. Truly, many of the people who failed in life are people who did not realize how close they were to their destiny fulfillment when they impatiently gave up and became victims of near success syndrome.

We must not struggle. I read a story of a certain farmer who never bothered to sort his potatoes the way others did after they were harvested. They were basically sorted into three categories: big, medium, and small for sales. While others painstakingly sorted and then loaded them in their trucks, he merely loaded his own unsorted and then took the roughest road to town. In the process, the potatoes just sorted themselves, with the little ones falling to the bottom, the medium to the middle, and the big ones rising to the top. The lessons are clear. In the tough times of life, we are made to rise to the top. We should not struggle to fulfill destiny; it will sort itself out.

YOUR BOAZ

Ruth may have been found by Naomi, but she still had to locate Boaz. While our Naomi must first locate us, we, on our part, must also be able to locate our Boaz; in the same sense, God gave us salvation, but we should work it out on our own (Phil 2:22).

Our Boaz may just be something of God's will for us that we need to work out in order to fulfill our destinies. It could be a holy living, or it may be a life partner or destiny helpers, and these, we must work out in accordance with God's plan for us if we must fulfill destiny.

To elaborate on this, we are told that Naomi came back with Ruth to Bethlehem at the beginning of the barley harvest. This entails that God will always make us to be part of the beginning of the foundational issues of life, for there is strength with the beginning. Tough men will naturally desire to surface when others have already suffered the foundation laying. It can't work as such and is contrary to the exemplary testimony of Paul to the Romans. He wrote, "Yea, so have I strives to preach the Gospel, not where Christ was named, lest I should build upon another man's foundation" (Rom. 15:20). Truly, better is the end of a matter, yet the same end is declared from the beginning. It's about beginnings (Isa. 46:10; Ecc. 7:8).

Now, there is always a Boaz that God has kept for everyone, and he can only be found by us in the place of humble service through hard work (Prov. 22:29). Even Ruth went and gleaned in the fields (Ruth 2:2).

This is a demonstration of service in humility. To glean means to pick up the grain left by the reapers. This, indeed, was, by law, the right of the poor to pick up the grain left by the reapers, as guaranteed by the law of Moses (Lev. 19:9-10; 23:22; Deut. 24:19). Ruth's humble desire and zeal to work were prompted by the harvest season and the desire to cater for her mother-in-law. Truly, we must humble ourselves for and in service. We must be willing to work. One of the greatest attacks against the church today is pride, and pride undermines true service. What we have in our churches are more crowds and fewer disciples, more miracle seekers and fewer miracle agents. Out of the few that serve, some are merely motivated by self, wanting to amass all to self; it's a syndrome of "me, myself and I"; the interest of others is void and such cannot bring fulfillment of destiny.

Ruth saw the harvest, and she was out-rightly moved, not minding the derogatory nature of it. Jesus, when He was moved by the harvest, said in two different instances or occasions in the Bible that the harvest is plenteous but laborers are few. The work of the kingdom in saving the wicked and the perishing world is increasing day by day, yet many are not humbly moved so much as to evangelize and serve or do the work of God in righteousness and humility.

While wickedness and unbelievers are growing in geometrical progression measure, service is relatively growing in arithmetical progression. There are more leaders who are merely raising followership than disciples and leaders. Jesus said, "follow me and I will make you fishers of men." This is twofold: follow and make. It's not just a request to follow. It's also that He will make. We are expected to preach and teach to the sinner and the saint respectively. Mark's message "to preach" in Mark 16:15 is targeted at the unbelieving gentiles who were to become believers, while Matthew's message in Matthew 28:20 to teach is targeted at the Jewish believers who were to be disciples. After conversion, service is necessary.

Ruth's desire to humbly and diligently work earned her a divinely induced connection with the great Boaz. You will surely locate your Boaz. Boaz was no doubt destined for Ruth, yet she needed to work diligently to have him. This is important and needs no emphasis.

Naomi means pleasant (love), while Boaz means "in Him is strength." This buttresses the fact that we can be found by His love (Naomi) in our Moab (world/sin), but we need to find His strength (Boaz) in His Bethlehem (His kingdom/the Church). This further implies that His love (Naomi) will locate us in our sinfulness, and we are to certainly locate His strength in service in His fold. This is also twofold: love and strength. His love qualifies us for His strength. It follows that this is the reason why many believers have not actually found and manifested strength in God, even after being born again for years. They think that the same manner in which we are saved will mean the way in which we can grow and be strong in the Lord. But truly, they are never the same. For our salvation, He gave us His son so that we can give ourselves back to His son.

Though we are saved by grace through faith, and not by works, yet by works, after we are first saved, can we be justified and keep our salvation (Eph. 2:8-9; Jam. 2:24-26).

You may not have seen or located your Boaz now, but through your good works, he will soon emerge. Praise God. This is true because Ruth actually met Boaz only after she had long labored or kept laboring and not just as she began to labor. The harvest is for an appointed time. In due season, it can never be too long, for a day is to God a thousand years, and a thousand years as a day. The devil may delay it due to our own faults or weaknesses, but it will eventually come to pass, if we make amends in our lives and of our weakness.

Like Ruth, soon after we've found our Boaz, we will not lack food, protection, or supplies (Ruth 2:11-14). All these are symbolic of strength, which Boaz represents. We must not give up. Ruth began and stayed in the work till the end. Don't just give up possibly because your Boaz has not noticed your hard work. In due season, it will come to pass (Ruth 1: 22, 2:23).

Importantly, Ruth saw the harvest (labor) as a divine providence and purpose for the discovering of her Boaz; we must see every opportunity to serve as a divine arrangement to promote and prosper us. We must not first desire monetary reward but work; we should not look for or desire Boaz but work. The problem with many is that we merely desire or look for our Boaz as per property, healing, miracles, favor, or payment, but not service, per se. We are not mainly called to earn but to serve.

"Even as the son of man came not to be ministered unto, but to minster without being paid or rewarded… A laborer is worthy of his wages" (1 Tim. 5:10). There can be pay without service, and a pay without service is just like receiving or earning what you didn't work for. It's like giving a person a fish without teaching them how to fish. We must also not selfishly see opportunity to serve as a means to be enslaved and be unduly used like the man that was given one talent in the parable of the talents (Matt. 25:14-30). The Bible says that we should even pray for those who despitefully use us (Matt. 5:44). Why? Because they may just be actually pointing us to our Boaz. Once again, every opportunity must never be easily despised and abandoned.

In God's kingdom work, those who don't work are replaced. May we not be replaced. Esther rose to the occasion when the Jews were under the threat of their lives by the realization that the defense of her people might just have been the purpose of her place in the palace. Listen, do the work or else another does it. Her destiny fulfillment was tied to the task of her delivering her fellow Jews from the onslaught of the enemy (Est. 4:12-14).

We are not called to be served, but to serve. Soon after we are saved and introduced to church, kingdom service must commence. Paul, soon after his salvation, inquired of the Lord, "What will you have me do?" Like Paul, you can ask the Lord the same, if you have not really been relevant in service. After salvation, it's discipleship. No talent should be withheld. People may go to hell because they refused to use their God-given talent to serve Him, that they withheld the gift. The man that was given one talent was cast into hell not for sin but for not using his gift (Matt. 25:14-30).

Finally, our strength is by service. Hence, through service Ruth found Boaz. Strength is life, and life is of God.

THE PLACE OF WISDOM

Naomi had found Ruth, and when Ruth had also found Boaz, Naomi then desired a home for Ruth (Ruth 3:1). It was, indeed, time for Ruth to have a home, a time for her to independently experience a mature and family life of rest.

Family life should be a secure or resting time in life, for God didn't actually mean it for struggles and regrets; that's never God's plan. This, He intended in the beginning – bringing the man and woman harmoniously together as one. And so wisdom was, indeed, a principal thing at this point of Ruth's destiny fulfillment and, of course, everyone who is born again and serving God in any capacity of gifting or calling (Prov. 4:7). Wisdom is practically the application of knowledge. In service, our salvation is put into practice. Ruth had dependently experienced so much. While we are being raised, our experiences are classified as dependent experiences, but when we are on our own, we rather get involved in an independent experience. Truly, realities of life are known to dawn on men in the latter. There, you are in the forefront. True assessment and judgement in life issues must not be based on the former. It's a transition. People don't see certain or core realities of life or ministry until they serve or are made to lead.

This applies to marriage as well. Our Christian strength will truly come to the test when we serve and serve well, indeed. So, Ruth had so much of dependent life experiences that it's clearly then time for the independent.

The problem with many marriages, ministries, or lives lies in the place of wisdom. Basically, dependent experience is like work knowledge, while our independent experiences have to do with actual work performance or practice. In other words, the dependent experiences are mainly things we apply in our independent experiences. So, in our independent life experiences, we must not discard our dependent life experiences. This is why training or stewardship is important and imperative. Master-hood is the application of servanthood. Beyond being trained, it is further important that one receives or stays in a good place of training, just as it is important that children are not just raised but are raised in a good home for the ripple effect.

Ruth's entire dependent life experiences with Naomi were pivotal to her readiness and maturity. And, subsequent to this, there was a plan for her to have a home. Of course, she had been found by Naomi, and she had also found Boaz. But, this was not to be the end. This is also where the problem of many marriages or ministries lies. We might have done it all, prayed and trusted so much for a life partner, but as soon as that is found, there it ends, little or no plan of making a home. For Ruth, after she was found and she fond Boaz, the next was a desire for a home and not just marriage, per se. What Naomi desired for her daughter-in-law was not just a husband but a home; there is a difference between both. Now, destiny fulfillment is a process, which encompasses dependent and independent stages of life experiences. If God has called us into ministry or any spheres of life with little or no plan on our own side in improving ourselves, then there can never be fulfillment. We might have found our Boaz or life partner but without a plan to raise or have a home. Soon after marriage, when real life challenge in this level of grace comes or begins to unfold, we can't stand it. It's one thing to find a partner; it's another to have a home. While the former is an outright individual affair, the latter is directly a collective phenomenon. It's a misconception to think or accept that discovering a partner automatically takes care of home making. This is the reason why many marriages are broken soon after wedlock. This must not be our portion. The vision and expectations of a couple should actually reflect the home making. A man and a woman must not get married without further knowing the clear career vision and expectations of each other. Ministries are often frustrated, not always because the call was not there, but because there was no sheer wisdom. Some businesses collapse not principally because they lack take off capital or personnel challenges but for lack of wisdom. The best of marriages fail because such were devoid of wisdom. We must earnestly pray for wisdom. We must go learn "how to do" after we've gotten the "knowledge" and are given "what to do". We must ASK God for wisdom. In fact, we are expected to ask for it (Jam. 1:5).

To connect and make herself ready and available to Boaz for marriage and life partnership, Naomi admonished Ruth to position herself well before

Boaz, whom she had long served. Great wisdom, indeed. Understand that Ruth means friendship. The saying goes thus: those who need friends must be friendly, a virtue which was paramount with Ruth in her strategy and wisdom in gaining Boaz. Ruth was to create a convenient time to present herself in such a way that Boaz must catch a great look and admiration of this destined lady who was to become his wife.

Naomi told Ruth to lie on the threshing floor where Boaz was to lay. Wisdom demands that there is time for everything, that we must be at the right place at the right time for a right purpose. Before now, it has been work; marriage was unconsciously in view. Oftentimes, we miss the mark because of an improper positioning. Being at the right position and at the right time can earn us an enormous advantage. May we, at all times, be in the right position at the right time. Blind Bartimaeus sat at the right path of Christ's movement. Consequently, he got his miraculous healing. Our allocation is often tied to our location. One must always place himself in a position of divine presence for liberty and victory (Ps. 16:11; 2 Cor. 3: 17; Ps. 68:2). The benefits of this may not be immediate, but like the lame man in Acts 3, it will someday come to pass. So long as we remain in the right location, irrespective of the delay or challenges. The same God who sent Peter and John will one day deliver to us that which God assigns for us.

It follows that Ruth was, by her mother-in-law, persuaded to "wash", anoint, and "dress up". Ruth was instructed by her mother-in-law to wisely prepare herself like a bride, a potential bride, indeed. Surely, preparations will precede actualization. What we don't prepare for, we don't accomplish. It's a demonstration of faith, a token of hope. Do you desire and dream to become anything? Then begin to look like it, and it will surely come to pass.

Ruth was to carry out this preparation of attractiveness. After which, she strategically positioned herself just after Boaz ate and drank. In other words, we must also patiently wait for Boaz to eat and drink before we position or make ourselves known. When we are sincerely attractive and friendly, we are bound to experience divine connection and attention for favor. The instruction of Naomi was quite strategic and thoughtful. Truly, this natural prescription translated into the spiritual.

Ruth was first to wash herself, which implies that she must first and foremost be clean. Based on my practical experience in marriage counseling, I have discovered that some couples often don't keep close and regular intimacy in bed because of unhygienic, filthy, or dirty personal habits of either husband or wife. This is spiritually symbolic, since until we are cleansed, we would not present ourselves to the Lord as saints and brides of the kingdom. After, we are discovered and brought out of our Moab, we must have ourselves spiritually cleansed by the word of God by growing in knowledge and application of the scripture (Eph. 5:26; Heb. 10:22; 2 Cor. 7:1; 1 Tim. 4:5; 1 Pt. 2:2).

It's a whole lot of a process of sanctification, a process in the sense that while salvation is instantaneous, sanctification remains continuous. We must continue to study and stay in His word as long as we live or He tarries.

Secondly, Ruth, after she had washed herself, was to further anoint herself; she was to perfume herself, indeed. This is important because it adds fragrance to the clean or washed body. It's like spicing or icing the cake; it preserves, keeps, or maintain freshness and tenderness of the clean body. This implies strength and its projects or announces a clean or washed body (Jn. 15). We must not only keep our body clean; an ointment or perfume should be added to announce such a clean body. It, of course, goes that this is with a clean body and must not be applied on an unclean body.

So it is also in the spiritual. We have many people who are holy or sanctified, and yet not anointed. Both are separate though integral or complementary. They can be experienced separate or at the same time at salvation. It's apparent in believers who are saved and holy but cannot win souls or do the work of God effectively. They lack divine strength to do the work of God. The disciples were born again, sanctified while they were first with Jesus, but were never yet announced abroad, not until the anointing of the Holy Ghost came on them (Acts 1:8).

There are practically many believers who are truly saved and holy, yet are not anointed, not baptized with the Holy Spirit even in the Pentecostal denomination. They can't just attract to real service. Paul saw this in the church of Ephesus; they were saved and sanctified but could not do exploits for Christ. Soon after hands were laid on them, they were baptized in the Spirit, and they began to do mighty works for the Lord. It is also important to understand the anointing can only be purely and genuinely effective after one is first saved, just as ointment or perfume should not be applied on a dirty body, else the fragrance of the perfume will be defiled, polluted, and deflected by the dirty odor of unclean or unwashed body. Anointing follows regeneration and purity, or cleanness.

The natural ointment or perfume is made to enhance and keep or preserve the clean body. No matter how well the body is washed, if it's not perfumed, especially in a temperate climate like ours, the freshness and odor will soon become unpleasant as we sweat. So also it is with our salvation and the anointing of the Holy Spirit. To regard perfume as carnal or sin is unscriptural, though moderation is essential.

Added to these was Naomi's dress up. Our dressing is our ultimate presentation, an outward feature. While the two others are not visible, her garment is visible. Our dressing tells so much of our inside from the outward. The way we dress, to a large extent, portrays how we are addressed. No matter how clean the body is washed and strongly perfumed or anointed, without clothing, it can be considered neither responsible nor sensible. We can't be clean and perfumed and then walk about naked without clothing. What this means in the spiritual context is that after we are saved and anointed, we must be responsible and of a good character. Charisma that lacks character is a catastrophe. Character is the outside of the inside quality of man. We must not only have Him dwell in us, we must also be clothed with Him. The Bible affirms that we are clothed with Christ. While our salvation and sanctification is symbolized by the physical washing, and the anointing of the Holy Spirit is natural perfuming, godly character is shown through physical adornment.

As these acts of threefold quality were potentially

present and qualified Ruth as a bride to Boaz, so also our salvation and sanctification, anointing and character, will present us as qualified bride to the Lord (Rev. 21:2).

After all these, Ruth was then admonished by Naomi to strategically wait until Boaz had finished eating and drinking for her to physically present herself before him. Wisdom, indeed! It was two sided. We must always consider others in all that we want to achieve. As it's good to be self-conscious, so also it's good to be considerate of others. Sometimes we make the mistake of thinking that because we are ready and prepared, others must be, too. And sometimes we even assess and judge others by our own point of readiness or fitness. We must further understand that often times, our readiness and preparedness does not mean God is ready and prepared for us; God's readiness for us does also mean that we are ready for him. This is where most callings come in conflict with God's plan. When we are ready, we must also wait for God to be ready for us, and when God is ready for us, we can wait until we are ready for Him. He is not in a haste. We must not just take off because we are ready. Ruth waited for the readiness of Boaz. And both came on at a point of agreement or harmony. It has nothing to do with ability and capability. Because you are not ready does not amount to inability. It's about timing and convenience.

Ruth was ready, Boaz had eaten, and she was introduced and presented herself. It's not enough to have all the requirements required, we must further make ourselves known and available. Because we are saved, holy, and anointed does not automatically mean God will compel us and impose responsibility on us. We must, further than that, be ready and willing to make ourselves known and available. We must, without deception and hypocrisy, offer ourselves to God for service and worship. This is the reason why we see some being used by God. It's about offering or presenting and making ourselves available to God (Rom. 12:1).

Some women of marriageable age sometimes think erroneously that the moment they are beautiful and possibly educated, a husband will automatically come. Those who think this way are greatly disappointed in their quest to marry. The truth is that we may have all the anointing and yet will not be used unless we readily offer ourselves. No matter how little we are anointed, if we make ourselves available, God is ever ready to use us mightily. God did not only desire to use His son, His son also offered Himself (Jn. 3:16; Gal. 2:21). Ruth offered herself to Boaz, not for immoral involvement and gratification, but for the purpose of fulfilling destiny.

Thus, from the beginning, we saw that Ruth had no problem accepting accordingly the advice and instructions of Naomi (Ruth 3:6).

The problem with many people in marriage, ministry, and careers lies with our avoidance of tactical advice or counsel on issues concerning this subject matter. If only we adhere to certain counsels in life, certain challenges would not exist or escalate.

While commending Ruth's adherence to Naomi, we must also draw a great lesson from Naomi's wise counsel and sense of responsibility toward Ruth's destiny and its fulfillment. As a leader, one must not only concentrate on providing followers with what they need but with what they can also do to get what they need on their own. We must not concentrate on performing miracles but teaching others how to perform the miracles. Naomi did not provide Ruth with Boaz, though she desired him for her; rather, she wisely taught and guided her on how to get the attention of Boaz. Leaders and parents must give room for independency of their followers, children, or wards when such needs arise. Any life experience while under a tutor only amounts to knowledge that must further be slated into wisdom. Real service is not when we operate dependently but independently. Initiative, discretion, and the ability to enhance are put to test in the latter. We are, at some certain points in life, dependent on others, in order to become independent in life in the future. The former is not an end but a means to achieving the latter. To stay on the former is to frustrate one's destiny fulfillment. Leaders who want others to continuously or permanently remain dependent on them are leaders who don't really want others to fulfill their destinies. Jesus did not merely gather men and transfer power to them to perform miracles, He taught them how to work out the miracles before they were sent out into the field. He said, "Follow me and I will make you become fishers of men." Note, the word, "make". He didn't say follow me and you will remain followers of me, but "I will make you become fishers of men". He launched the net, and He asked Peter to follow suit. There are two types of leaders: leaders whose principle is "follow me and you will remain followers of me," and leaders whose principle is "follow me and I will make you fishers of men". Naomi, indeed, fulfilled the latter in Ruth's path for fulfilling her destiny.

THE PLACE OF HUMILITY

Humility is essential to fulfilling destiny. It's simply the absence of pride. Pride sinks and aborts destiny fulfillment.

After Boaz had eaten and was happy, he went to lie down at the end of the heap of corn. There, Ruth went wisely and softly and uncovered his feet and laid down at his feet, a clear demonstration of humility, an outright revelational symbol of a true heart of humility. That she lay at his feet was motivated by a clear, sheer heart of humility and not immorality. Thus, staying at the feet of the Lord in like manner indicates an act of humility to receive of Him in His presence. There at his feet, Boaz took notice of Ruth's presence. Her humility based on her actions brought about Boaz's corresponding humility. One good turn, they say, deserves another. God is never moved by our actions, services, or worship when they are full of pride and ego. Some of us, left to our own devices, would be motivated by the desire of being on top to attract attention to ourselves, instead of waiting patiently for our divine unveiling time and season.

Boaz was likely moved by Ruth's humble posture and submission there at his feet, coupled with her humble request. People feel respected and positively moved by humble requests of others. Hence, Boaz needed to listen and know more about her. "Ruth your handmaid" she humbly responded to his request of who she was, as she formally requested for an intimate share of warmness, comfort, and for him to make his claim on her as her kinsman redeemer. Ruth saw Boaz as a security, a covering, a husband by faith; she had found rest or home in him, as earlier envisaged by Naomi (Ruth 3:1). Interestingly, Ruth's request that Boaz should spread his skirt over her, his handmaid, was symbolic of a marriage proposal initiative and acted in wisdom, faith, and humility (Ruth 3:9).

This is great lesson for unmarried sisters. The truth is that there are some men who are interested in marrying certain sisters but can't approach such sisters. They just stay around them and are kind to them directly or indirectly, and yet, no marriage moves. Such sisters must not keep quiet in such situations if their hearts concur. In humility, they can prayerfully, boldly, and wisely initiate and make the moves themselves. They must not wait unnecessarily. Such sisters, if they find it difficult to take this initiative, can seek counseling from appropriate counselors. Many have been helped in this regard and, by the grace of God, they all ended in marriage. It's also important for sisters, especially of marriageable age, to settle the motive and bases of every man that closely and personally wants to relate with them. If the brother is not forth coming in explaining his motives or mission, the sister should ask him. It's possible, those men are being used by the devil to block the chance of the genuine and serious man. No responsible man would want to ask the hand of a sister in marriage when another brother is pestering and hovering around her. They just come to divert the real man.

Truly, we must, like Ruth, make our request in wisdom, humility, and faith. It's not in the asking, per se, but in the presentation of the request. The wise and the humble will always have their request met both by men and God. I dare to say that such people will often not lack. They can't die in silence. Ruth saw Boaz as her husband by faith. She called a thing that was not as though it were. God is to us what we, by faith, take or see Him to be to us. The strength of what He is to us is directly determined by the value we place on Him in our lives. Now this, however, does not actually negate who He is, irrespective of the value we place on Him. Whenever we demonstrate true faith, heaven establishes our desires and expectations.

It's about expectation. "The expectation of the righteous shall not be cut off", which the Bible affirms. We are commanded to ask in faith (Jam. 1:6). Ruth's marriage to Boaz was fundamentally prophetic and destined. Prophecy is the eyes that see the destined future. Both prophecy and destiny are in agreement and do not contradict one another. Ruth's humility no doubt instigated Boaz's interest, which eventually brought her destiny to prophetic fulfillment. Boaz only played into destiny, in which control compelled him to key into humbling himself in marrying Ruth. Wisdom, humility, and faith can break the strongest of the pride of men for our ultimate destiny fulfillment. Ruth's humility and hard work in providing for Naomi further earned her mother-in-law's assurance in her hope of Ruth marrying Boaz, Naomi's kinsman. We must not forget those the Lord is using on our way to fulfilling destiny. We must work hard and share with them the fruit of our labor. This gesture is, as well, a product of humility.

We should not run away from trials and sufferings, for these can create in us obedience, patience, and humility. Christ, the Bible says, learned obedience through suffering. On the path of fulfilling His destiny on earth, He had to go up to Jerusalem, and there He suffered many things in the hands of men and authorities and was even killed but raised again on the third day. He had to do so if He was to fulfill His destiny. We must not promote anything that will deny us a humble experience. Soon after Christ had announced His bitter and derogatory experience of shame, Peter then "fleshly" opposed Him, refusing that the exalted one should suffer shame. But the ways of God are not the ways of men. For Him to be exalted, He had to be humbled; to be humbled is to be exalted.

In all this, Jesus knew the consequences of exposing His exalted position and status at that point in time. Knowing quite well that if the enemy had known Him as Christ, then they may refrain from attacking Him, and that would have hindered our redemption and the fulfillment of His destiny. To wisely and humbly conceal His status, He began by asking his disciples who others thought He was. John's report to this simply indicated that the people (Jews) had no exact comprehension of His exalted identity. In His effort to settle this issue, He further threw the question directly to His disciples themselves, and this time Peter answered that He was the Christ. Upon this right revelation of his identity, He therefore commanded them to tell no man about the reality of His identity, that it must be kept until an appointed time. He must first suffer, be rejected and slain, and be raised on the third day before His divine unveiling.

The lesson here is emphatically revealing and important. What it teaches is that if we must have the opportunity and privilege of going through certain trials or tests that will enhance our destiny fulfillments, we must first humble ourselves. The disciples were asked to keep this revelation simply because if the people knew Him to be the exalted one of God, then certainly they would not have suffered, rejected, and killed Him. Such an exalted status, if disclosed, would hinder His trials and murder, "for had they known, they would not have crucified the Lord of glory" (1 Cor. 2:8).

This is the place and importance of humility in destiny fulfillment. Humility does not really undermine exaltation; it only enhances fulfillment of destiny for our eternal exaltation. It really took humility for Christ to have humbled Himself to face those derogatory situations. There are certain achievements, positions, statuses, and prestige that we experience—trials that may earn us heavenly glory and exaltation. We may not have experienced certain humble trials that will divinely exalt us to glory because of our self-exaltation and pride. We have made ourselves highly esteemed by men and exaltation in due time, and such was the testimony of Ruth (1 Pt. 5:5-6).

Truly, God resists the proud (Jam. 4:6).

Ruth's secret of grace, by which she captured the sincere attention of Boaz, can be attributed to her humble spirit. She humbled herself, and she was ultimately exalted (Lk. 14;11).

THE PLACE OF FAVOR

Favor is unspeakably essential to destiny and its fulfillment. It can't be neglected. It's a driving force. Even with wisdom and humility, we still require favor. It worked for Ruth. She sought for Boaz's favor (Ruth 2:13). Jesus Christ needed favor to fulfill the father's will on Earth (Lk. 2:52). Favor is needed both from God and man. Hence, Ruth desired Boaz's favor. We must seek it, though God's favor will command the favor of man.

Favor is simply help, approval, and support. We are creatures of divine favor, as the peak and crown of all creatures (Gen. 1: 26, 28).

There are three areas of favor in life, and these, of course, are the major areas of satanic and demonic interest and attack against us.

First, the favor of wife and husband (Prov. 18:22). A good wife is what every man must desire and look forward to having. A wife is a great channel of God's favor to a man or home. Without a wife, there is no favor, and it's not good for any man to live without favor (Gen. 2:18). Some women face a long period of preparatory challenges before marriage because God must transform them into virtue of favor for His sons.

A man who is fulfilled in his career or business is a man who is favored by God with a good wife. Jezebel stirred her husband into wicked works (1 Kn. 21:25). Her name meant "unmarried". She ruined her husband's partner–Naboth (1 Kn. 21). She also destroyed her husband's friendship with Jehoshaphat (2 Chro. 18). She was a bad wife with whom there was no favor. A bad wife will birth unfavorable situations in a home. A woman's moment of disfavor can amount to a great damage, and such was the case of Eve, through whom the entirety of humanity was plunged into disobedience and sin (Gen. 3:1; 1 Cor. 11: 3; 1 Tim. 2:14). This can happen at any stage of a married life. There should not be detachment in marriage, both spiritually and physically, a disconnection of favor. This was what evil needed in order to attack, to detach Adam from his wife. Hence, a cloud of darkness came before them by way of the devil's deception and the consequent nakedness and shame that befell them (Gen. 3).

The second type of favor is in life (Ps. 30:5). The Bible affirms that God's favor, which preserves life, is tantamount to fulfilling destiny. We are not permitted to die without fulfilling destiny. He created "man", not baby or child–these are mainly processes of attaining the stature of a man which we are in creation (Gen. 1:26). And so we must not die in this process. It's an abomination. Our life must not be cut short by forces of any means. Nothing can be compared to fulfilled days of God's life expectancy for man on earth. It's a demonstration and proof of his salvation (Ps. 91:16).

Life is a function of our destiny. Every man's life

span is patterned by God to the extent that he can fulfill his destiny. We buy products and we are given guarantees; in other words, such products must fulfill their expected days or time in service or use. The greatest loss is that of losing a man, through strange forces, to death before his set time (Heb. 2:14-15). We must resist it. For this purpose, you may need to call on God now (2 Kn. 20:1-6).   Thirdly, favor is victory over enemies (Dt. 33:23). Favor will command victory over enemies in battle. With favor, we are assured of victory in every battle of life we fight. And we must not lose a battle, for every lost battle will have a negative generational effect. Thus, victory is a sign of God's favor upon a man. Determine not to lose a battle–fight on as a man. You have an oil of favor poured on you by the Holy Ghost (Isa. 41:13). All these aided Ruth's victory in her great battles of life in fulfilling destiny.

PROVIDENCE

Providence is a divine force that controls our life and the things that happen to us in the course of fulfilling destiny. It is connected to destiny; it's destiny's controlling factor, which drives destiny.

In destiny, there isn't anything like luck. Luck is not a biblical word and, therefore, does not apply to believers. The word luck merely has to do with chance, while providence is a truly assured divine occurrence in the process of fulfilling destiny and not an accidental phenomenon or outcome of luck.

So, providentially, all was set for Ruth to ultimately get married to a kinsman to that effect. This request was duly presented in line with the tradition of the land to the nearest kinsman who, based on providence of destiny, rejected the offer. Therefore, there was none other than Boaz to fit into the trend of Ruth's destiny fulfillment. Before the nearest kinsman was available, there was the offer of buying the field which Naomi had put up for sale, along with the traditional requirement of marrying Ruth, Mahlon's widow in order to maintain the name of the dead (Ruth 4:1-10).

The revelational implication of redemption of the field alongside marrying Ruth is significant. This implies that Christ did not only pay for our sins but also has acquired us to Himself in a heavenly marriage. Two things are involved here: paying for our sins and divinely getting married to us. Now, the problem, therefore, is in yielding ourselves for this relationship and not because our sin has not been paid for.

The rejection of the nearer kinsman made it providently possible for Boaz, the next kinsman, who then was able and willing to pay for the redemption of the field and, as well, get married to Ruth (Ruth 4:1-5). Together, Boaz and Ruth fulfilled the great destiny of bringing forth the seed of the future kings. The will of God will always prevail (Matt. 6:10).

If we work in obedience to God in fulfilling our destiny, we will not need to worry nor panic over life. Ruth was destined to marry Boaz and that had long been in process divinely. Providence will have to play its course; hence, the nearer kinsman would on his own accord certainly give way. Nothing of God is accidental or magical. We don't need to truncate the due process, for what God has made for us, remains for us. The problem with most men is that they try to shortcut, fast track, and eliminate certain stages or points in fulfilling destiny, and it must not be so.

Ruth and the rest had done their part of the mission; it was left to God to perfect His own side. When we humbly apply wisdom in line with our destiny, men will be ready to sacrifice all for us. We will not struggle. Providence took its course, and Boaz ultimately got married to Ruth (Ruth 4:13).

We will not be threatened in fulfilling destiny. God will always help us in life's choices and the transitional situations we will encounter as we fulfill our destiny. He will uphold our positive choices and obedience as they affect our destiny fulfillment. God's ultimate help, based on our godly wisdom and humility in fulfilling destiny, which will surely translate into great joy and praises for a destiny well fulfilled.

Boaz's marriage to Ruth brought forth Obed, meaning "service," which suggests and portrays the life of service in Ruth. This brought to pass the greatest ancestral process of the savior: Obed had Jesse had David, which led to a clear lineage of Christ (Ruth 4:17-24; Matt. 1). This is an ultimate fulfillment of destiny (Ruth 4:13 -22).

CONCLUSION

Destiny is real and its fulfillment is not a mirage. Fulfillment of destiny is a journey of life. Ruth came a long way to fulfilling her destiny. Her journey of destiny fulfillment was clear; it was not an abstract issue. Ruth's life is a model of destiny fulfillment, a pattern for us to be guided and courageously fulfill our own destiny.

First, it was Naomi getting Ruth, and then Ruth getting Boaz. While Naomi means pleasant or love, Boaz means strength. In between these two points were trials of destiny fulfillment. In a spiritual connotation, it implies that between the time when we are born again and called and when we obtain by grace the strength of God, there come some trials.

These are basically two levels of grace every man will experience for eternity. The love of God is first, and His strength is second. Apparently, everyone needs Naomi and Boaz, love and strength, respectively. And both the love and strength of God will produce service. Obed, the product of the union, means service. To serve God, we must be saved and anointed or filled by the Holy Ghost.

Wisdom, humility, favor and providence are also essential factors in fulfilling destiny. I hereby declare, thus:

i. That your Naomi will never find rest in her Bethlehem–Judah until you are located in your Moab

ii. That she will count it worthy to sacrifice all for your sake

iii. That you will work the work that will connect you to your Boaz

iv. That you will locate your Boaz who then will, in turn, get connected to your destiny fulfillment

v. That God will grant you the grace for wisdom, humility, and providence in fulfilling your destiny

vi. That your destiny will surely be fulfilled, and that you will be part of the history of Christ Jesus' kingdom on earth

Note: you can further translate these declarations into prayers, decrees, and meditation for proper appropriation.

ABOUT THE AUTHOR

Pastor Mba Stewart is an author, teacher, trainer, and the senior pastor of Priesthood Assembly Inc. He is a theologian and church administration and management expert. As the president of Christian Training Services, he has had the opportunity to train and mentor many pastors and church leaders. He holds a first degree in Marketing, and a doctorate degree in Theology (Church administration and management). Pastor Stewart is married to Aderomola, and they are blessed with five children.

Pastor Mba may be reached through e-mail:
mbastewart@yahoo.com,
or
http://www.priesthood.50webs.org/index.html

EDITOR'S NOTE

This book qualifies for publisher's One-for-One Challenge. Buy a copy, and publisher will donate $1 dollar to establish resource centers for orphanages in developing countries, where these amazing kids may learn to read, dream, and grow. Just because they are orphans doesn't mean their future has to be limited. Learn more at www.kharispublishing.com

As a social enterprise, Kharis Publishing has a two-fold mission: giving voice to underrepresented authors (including women, minorities, internationals, and first-time authors) to publish their books free of charge; and empowering orphans through literacy initiatives. Kharis Publishing also welcomes corporate partnerships with churches, libraries, schools, business corporations, and individuals.

www.ingramcontent.com/pod-product-compliance
Lightning Source LLC
LaVergne TN
LVHW051421080426
835508LV00022B/3192